I0081652

RESTORED

A Story of Grace, Grit, and Growth

VIVIAN YAKPO-NEWTON

LUCIDBOOKS

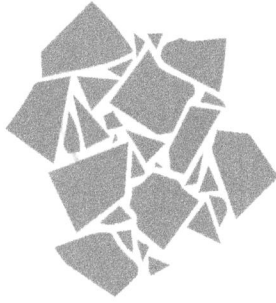

Like stained glass, this story is made of fragments, shattered moments, sharp edges, and colorful pieces of a life reassembled by grace. Each broken piece holds a memory, a lesson, a triumph, Together, they create something whole. Something radiant. This is not just a memory, it is a mosaic. And in its light, you'll see the beauty of becoming.

Restored: A Story of Grace, Grit, and Growth
Copyright © 2026 by Vivian Yakpo-Newton
Published by Lucid Books in Houston, TX
www.LucidBooks.com

All rights reserved. No part of this publication may be reproduced, stored in a retrieval system, or transmitted in any form by any means, electronic, mechanical, photocopy, recording, or otherwise, without the prior permission of the publisher, except as provided for by USA copyright law.

Unless otherwise indicated, scripture quotations are taken from the Holy Bible, New International Version®, NIV®. Copyright ©1973, 1978, 1984, 2011 by Biblica, Inc.™ Used by permission of Zondervan. All rights reserved worldwide. www.zondervan.com The "NIV" and "New International Version" are trademarks registered in the United States Patent and Trademark Office by Biblica, Inc.™

Scripture quotations marked (ESV) are taken from the ESV® Bible (The Holy Bible, English Standard Version®), copyright © 2001 by Crossway, a publishing ministry of Good News Publishers. Used by permission. All rights reserved.

Scripture quotations marked (KJV) are taken from the King James Version (KJV): King James Version, public domain.

Scripture quotations marked (NKJV) are taken from the New King James Version®. Copyright © 1982 by Thomas Nelson. Used by permission. All rights reserved.

ISBN: 978-1-63296-890-6
ISBN: 978-1-63296-946-0 (hardback)
eISBN: 978-1-63296-892-0

Special Sales: Most Lucid Books titles are available in special quantity discounts. Custom imprinting or excerpting can also be done to fit special needs. Contact Lucid Books at Info@LucidBooks.com

To Kwame and Kwesi—
my sons, my strength, my greatest gifts.

This book is for you.
For the nights we stayed up late.
For the prayers we whispered together.
For the laughter that broke through tears.
For the faith that carried us through.

You have been my reason to rise,
my joy in the struggle, and my evidence that
love and grace can rewrite any story.

Thank you for walking this journey with me.
I am who I am because of you.
You are my legacy.

TABLE OF CONTENTS

PROLOGUE

Our story started like a beautiful tale filled with love and laughter. Each moment felt special, ready to become a cherished memory. I always dreamed of a life filled with love, success, and exciting adventures, where we could explore the world together. However, life took unexpected turns, leading me toward an uncertain future that I never expected. The dreams I once held so dearly began to drift like autumn leaves caught in a gust of wind, leading me down a road marked by unforeseen challenges and revelations. What I once deemed a straightforward journey transformed into a web of emotions, testing the very foundations of my aspirations and beliefs. Becoming a single parent was a reality I never imagined facing, a challenge thrust upon me after the unexpected end of a long-term relationship and marriage. It was a profound test of endurance, resilience, and love, one that demanded more from me than I ever thought possible. In the aftermath of heartbreak, when the world felt heavy and overwhelming, I discovered an inner strength I never knew I possessed. Day by day, I took on the dual role of both mom and dad, learning to juggle school runs, bedtime stories, and playdates, all while managing the financial responsibilities that now rested solely on my shoulders. I faced sleepless nights filled with worry and doubt, yet I carried the load of this new responsibility with a fierce determination and love for my boys.

Each challenge transformed into an opportunity for growth, forging an unbreakable bond between us as we learned to navigate this new chapter of our lives together.

My sons, Kwame and Kwesi, are the very essence of my life and my greatest joys. Kwame, my eldest, embodies my sense of self and determination, always stepping up as a role model not just for his younger brother but also within our community. On the other hand, Kwesi possesses a creative spirit that brings boundless energy and delightful surprises to our daily lives. Together, we have faced various challenges, from the ups and downs of school life to personal setbacks that have tested our resilience. Yet, through every trial, I have always strived to cultivate a nurturing environment brimming with unconditional love, faith, and a spirit of perseverance that binds us together as a family. Our home is often filled with laughter, heartfelt discussions, and shared moments of reflection. Despite the challenges we encountered, I made it a priority to teach them the importance of empathy toward others, the value of persistence during tough times, and the necessity of having faith in God's grace to guide us through. I want them to grow into compassionate and resilient individuals who understand the significance of community and kindness. As a family, we gather for weekly movie nights and volunteer together at local shelters, reinforcing our commitment to these values in tangible ways. A new chapter awaited us as we boarded a plane bound for the United States, stepping into an uncertain future. This is not a story of perfection, but a testament to love's triumph, the power of resilience, and the unbreakable bond between a mother and her sons.

To every single parent reading this, especially those quietly carrying the weight of dreams deferred, know this: you are not alone. The road is rarely smooth, and often it feels like no one sees the work you do in the quiet hours, the sacrifices, the small victories, or the weariness behind your smile. But your strength is not hidden, and your love—steady, fierce, and deep—is shaping lives in ways that will echo for generations. Keep going. Even on the hardest days, you are building something beautiful. This story is for you, too.

This is our journey.

Chapter One

WHEN THE BOTTOM FALLS OUT

"Weeping may endure for a night,
but joy comes in the morning."
— Psalm 30:5 (NKJV)

In autumn, Heidelberg transforms into a breathtaking tapestry of colors, with vibrant oranges, rich gold, and deep browns painting the landscape like an artist's masterpiece. In our backyard, my two boys rode their bicycles, their laughter bubbling forth like effervescent streams of joy, filling the crisp air with an infectious spirit. They moved through the fallen leaves, their faces bright with joy. They showed a carefree innocence that sharply contrasted with the heavy feelings I was experiencing. As I stood at the edge of the yard with my arms crossed tightly against my chest, I felt as if I were trying to shield myself from the painful truth that loomed over me like dark storm clouds. Tears slowly trickled down my cheeks, creating a silent testament to the heartache I could no longer conceal.

The previous night replayed in my mind like a haunting melody, a memory I desperately wished I could escape. My husband and I sat across from our pastors in the dimly lit church office, where the air hung thick with unspoken tension. The soft glow from the flickering candle cast long shadows on the walls, amplifying the sense of unease that enveloped us. I had hoped for a breakthrough or perhaps a sign of reconciliation, something to ease the burden that had settled between us. Instead, his words crashed over me like a sudden storm. "I want a divorce," he stated flatly, his voice devoid of warmth, leaving an icy silence in their wake. The finality of his declaration echoed in my mind, intertwining with the colorful beauty of the autumn landscape, as my heart ached to comprehend the reality of our shattered dreams.

He dismissed any idea of counseling. His determination remained strong, even as the shock on the pastors' faces and my own was clear. My pastor wanted to understand, so he asked for an explanation. My husband stayed quiet, looking off into the distance. This created a deep sense of sadness in the room. The walls seemed to close in around me, and my breath was shallow as my world spun out of control. I excused myself, the need for escape overwhelming, and locked myself in the tiny bathroom down the hall. My knees hit the cold tile floor with a thud, and the floodgates of tears opened. "God, what am I going to do?" I cried, my voice trembling as the weight of uncertainty pressed down on me. How could I raise two boys on my own? How would I manage without completing my college degree, without a plan, without him? The questions tumbled over one another in my mind, each more suffocating than the last. After what felt like an eternity, I splashed cold water on my face, trying to wash away the evidence of my despair.

The reflection staring back at me in the mirror was almost unrecognizable, a woman on the brink of collapse. Yet, I forced myself to draw in a deep breath and stand. I had to go back to face him, the pastors, and the unraveling of my life. When I returned, the room was thick with a quiet awkwardness. The pastors' faces were kind but pained. Their words of comfort, meant to soothe and reassure, were tinged with an unmistakable sense of helplessness, revealing the deep empathy in their eyes as they struggled to find the right phrases. Heavy with unspoken sorrow, each syllable seemed to hang in the air as they offered their support, knowing full well that some pain cannot be alleviated by mere words alone. They gathered around me, their hands warm and comforting as they prayed, their voices blending into a steady chorus that cut through the chaos in my mind. Each word of support resonated deeply, enveloping me like a warm hug and easing the turmoil in my heart. But when we stepped out of the church that night, the cold air was a sharp contrast to the warmth inside, and I could feel a heavy silence settling between my husband and me. It carried an unspoken weight, full of fears and emotions we hadn't addressed, looming over our future like a dark cloud. The road ahead stretched out, twisted and uncertain, with familiar signs of hope slipping farther away.

The journey back home was a long and silent one, each minute stretching into what felt like hours. The rhythmic hum of the car engine filled the void between us, yet it did little to mask the suffocating tension that hung like a heavy curtain in the air. As we pulled into the driveway, the headlights flooded the dimly lit path, illuminating the scattered remnants of our shared life. He wasted no time moving his belongings out of our once-cozy bedroom into the guest room. The finality of his actions hit me like a punch to the gut, leaving me breathless and stunned. I went to check on our sleeping boys, admiring their innocent faces. The stark contrast between their peaceful slumber and the turmoil that had unfolded just a few hours earlier felt overwhelming. I said goodnight to the babysitter and forced a weak smile that didn't reach my eyes, hiding the mix of emotions inside me. When the house grew quiet and still, I went to my room. It now felt like an unfamiliar space, stripped of the warmth and comfort it once held. My mind raced with endless questions that crashed through the silence: "Why is this happening to me?" "How could someone leave their marriage without an explanation?" Each thought echoed off the walls, making me feel even more alone. I lay in bed and tried to sleep, but sleep eluded me.

The night dragged on, each hour stretching into what felt like an eternity, as the clock ticked cruelly in the dim light of my bedroom. I sobbed quietly, breaking the silence around me. Tears streamed down my face, soaking my pillow. The dampness was a physical manifestation of my inner turmoil. I found it hard to understand how we ended up in this empty place. Love once thrived here, but now it felt like a distant memory.

Clinging to prayer like a lifeline, I sank deeper into my thoughts, my heart racing with desperation. I pleaded with God for divine intervention, for a miracle to save my marriage, to grant me clarity in the chaos, and to fortify me with the strength I desperately needed to face whatever lay ahead. The weight of my fears pressed heavily upon my chest as I searched for answers in the darkness, hoping for a flicker of hope to guide me through this overwhelming despair. As I lay awake that night, memories of laughter, shared dreams, and the vibrant community we had built played like a reel in my mind. It was hard to reconcile those moments of joy with the cold reality I now face. How had we gone from our life so full of promise to this fractured marriage and an uncertain future? The questions remained unanswered as the first light of dawn crept through the curtains, signaling the start of another day in a world that felt irrevocably changed.

Chapter Two

THE BREAKING POINT: WHEN TRUTH SHATTERS TRUST

*"The Lord is close to the brokenhearted and saves
those who are crushed in spirit."*
— Psalm 34:18 (NIV)

The morning after my husband asked for a divorce, I stood motionless in the living room, staring out the large glass window. The crisp autumn air seeped through the cracks, carrying with it the faint scent of fallen leaves. Outside, the vibrant foliage drifted gently to the ground, a quiet reminder of change. Inside, I felt a hollow numbness, as if the chill of the approaching winter had already settled deep within me. The previous night replayed in my mind; each word and gesture etched vividly into my memory. My husband and I stayed in this very room, the same living room where we had shared countless moments of joy and laughter, where we had hosted friends, celebrated holidays and birthdays, and spent quiet, content evenings. But last night, the air was thick with tension when we sat down with our pastors. The weight of his words sank like stones in the pit of my stomach. I had known something was wrong, but nothing could have prepared me for what followed. "I want a divorce." The words had hung in the air, a chasm opening between us, impossible to bridge. I stared at him, my mind struggling to process the reality of what he had just said. My heart had pounded in my chest, a painful, erratic rhythm that echoed the shattering of my world.

Standing alone now in the morning light, I felt the weight of his words settle into my bones. The man I had built my life with, my partner, my confidant, had made a decision that shattered the foundation of everything I thought we had. As I gazed through the window, the autumn leaves drifted downward, carried by the wind's whim before coming to rest on the earth. Each leaf was a mirror of my own sense of loss, beautiful in their descent, yet detached from the branches they once clung to. Our marriage, once so full of life and promise, now seemed as broken as those scattered leaves. The question I kept asking myself was: When did it all begin to fall apart? It was an evening like any other when he returned from a trip to Tanzania with one of our church friends. Yet, something about him was different. His movements through the house were subtle but distant, a shift I couldn't quite name.

That night, I felt a tight knot in my stomach that kept me from sleeping. I got out of bed, and the quiet house felt heavy around me. I walked to the study, where the dim light from the desk lamp made long shadows, creating a strange atmosphere. I settled into my familiar leather chair. As I fiddled with the clutter of papers and books scattered across the desk, my gaze landed on something unusual—a stack of photographs carelessly abandoned in the corner. I felt a tightness in my throat as I reached for them, and a feeling of fear came over me. With trembling fingers, I began to flip through the images, and each one felt like a piercing stab to my heart. Each photograph unveiled explicit shots of a woman I had trusted deeply—a close family friend, part of both our African circles and our church community, a married woman with a husband who adored her. The intimate nature of the pictures left me reeling, my mind racing as the crushing weight of betrayal sank in, and I couldn't find the words to express how I felt. How could this cherished figure, who had shared laughter and meals with my family, betray the very values we upheld? I felt a mixture of disbelief and anger boiling within me, leaving me rooted to that spot, unable to process the enormity of what I had discovered. My body began to tremble as the truth unfolded before me. Why would she give these to my husband? Why would he accept them? And what would her husband think? Suddenly, the pieces clicked together! His request for a divorce, his distance, his late nights—they were all tied to her.

The next day, my husband left early for our church picnic. I couldn't keep my discovery inside any longer. I had to confront her. My heart pounded as I picked up the phone and dialed her number, my hands trembling. When she answered, her voice was calm and familiar, but I could hear the shift when she realized it was me.

"Hello?" she said.

"Why?" My voice cracked. "Why did you do it?"

There was a pause, then a sharp intake of breath. "Do what?" she asked, feigning ignorance.

"Don't play games with me," I said, my throat tightening. "You know what I'm talking about. You betrayed me. I trusted you."

Her response hit me like a slap. "Don't blame me for your failed marriage."

Her voice was cold, sharp, and unapologetic. I sat there, frozen, struggling to process the cruelty of her response.

She was someone I had trusted, and from the moment we met, I welcomed her into my home without hesitation. She sat at my table, shared meals with my family, and laughed with us as if she truly belonged. When she needed help, I was there. Whether it was a kind word, a prayer, or a shoulder to lean on, I gave freely because I believed she was my sister—not by blood, but by faith. We worshiped together, so I thought we stood on the same foundation, guided by the same beliefs. Never, not even once, did I imagine she would betray me in such a painful way. It wasn't just a betrayal of friendship; it was a deep wound, one that cut through the trust I had built in her. My mind raced back to the times I trusted her with my husband during their trip to Africa. I had felt safe then, confident that our shared beliefs were a shield against betrayal. But as I sat here now, the truth was raw and undeniable.

My marriage had not ended because of my flaws or mistakes. It ended because of their choices, not mine. She had made her choice and so had he. And now, in this painful moment, I realized I had a choice to make too. A single tear escaped and slid down my cheek. I wiped it away quickly; glad she couldn't see me through the phone. My voice trembled as I spoke. "I hope you never have to feel what I feel right now," I said softly.

The line went silent. I waited a moment, then hung up.

My heart was heavy with sorrow but also with a strange sense of clarity. The road ahead would be long and difficult. There would be endless conversations, legal proceedings, and the painful task of dividing a life we had built together. The dreams we once shared were gone, casualties of a marriage that couldn't survive the weight of betrayal.

I took a deep breath and put the phone down. I didn't know exactly how I would navigate the journey ahead, but I knew one thing for sure: I was done standing still in the shadow of their choices. It was time to start reclaiming my life, one step at a time.

The phone rang, and I checked the caller ID. It was my friend Helen. My hands trembled as I picked up the phone.

"Hello?" I answered, my voice shaky.

"Vivian? What's wrong?" Helen asked, concern evident in her voice.

I tried to speak, but the words got stuck. A sob escaped my lips.

"Are you okay?" she asked again, more urgently this time.

Through my tears, I finally managed to whisper, "My husband asked for a divorce last night."

"What?" she exclaimed. "Why?"

"He's having an affair."

"I'm coming over right now. Is he home?" Helen's voice was firm and determined.

"No," I said softly. "He already left for the church picnic."

"I'm on my way," she said and hung up.

When Helen arrived, she found me sitting in the garden with tears streaming down my face. She wrapped her arms around me, and we stood there in silence. Her embrace gave me the strength I didn't know I had left.

"Come on," she said gently. "Let's get you dressed. We're going to the picnic."

"I can't," I protested. "I don't want anyone to see me like this."

"It will be good for you," she insisted. Her eyes showed both determination and compassion.

Realizing I wasn't going to win this battle, I reluctantly agreed. As I dressed my sons, tears continued to stream down my face. My eldest, just five years old, noticed.

"Mommy, why are you crying?" he asked, his innocent eyes full of concern.

"Mommy just doesn't feel well," I answered, forcing a smile.

Helen drove us to the park; the car filled with the soothing sounds of praise and worship songs. She prayed for me as we traveled, asking God to give me peace and strength.

Every year, our church in Mannheim looked forward to the annual picnic, a cherished tradition that brought everyone together for a day of fun, fellowship, and food. The weather that Sunday was perfect, with a gentle autumn breeze stirring the vibrant, golden leaves. Volunteers had arrived early to set up tables and chairs, string colorful bunting between the trees, and arrange bouquets of flowers.

When we stepped out of the car, the delicious aroma of grilled meats and freshly baked pastries greeted us. The laughter and chatter of church members filled the air, mingling with the delighted squeals of children enjoying games and activities. My eldest, Kwame, ran ahead to the bouncy castle. His little brother, Kwesi, tried to keep up but couldn't match his brother's speed.

I spotted my husband across the park, smiling and welcoming the boys with open arms. My heart ached, but I forced a polite smile for the others around me. I kept my sunglasses on, hoping they would hide the redness and swelling from my tears.

"Are you okay?" one of the ladies asked gently.

"Just not feeling like myself today," I replied, sitting down with a few of the women I trusted. I shared a bit of my heartache, and they listened with empathy. Helen squeezed my hand and whispered a prayer for strength.

The assistant pastor approached me later, his expression kind. "Vivian," he said softly, "the pastors told me what happened."

I nodded, unable to speak as tears trickled from beneath my sunglasses.

"Don't let this situation make you cynical," he continued. "You are a kind and joyful person. Don't let the enemy rob you of that."

"Thank you," I whispered.

I turned back to watch my boys play, their laughter mingling with the sounds of the picnic. At that moment, I realized that even though my world was falling apart, there were still glimpses of light. And with faith, support, and time, I might just find my way through the storm. My friends' support meant the world to me, and I made sure to express my deep gratitude for their kindness. As the day began to wind down, we said goodbye to all and headed home. When we arrived home, I thanked Helen for ensuring the safety of myself and my boys by insisting that I not drive on the autobahn in my condition. After bidding her farewell as she departed, I carried my youngest, Kwesi, and held onto Kwame's hand as we descended the stairs into our home.

Chapter Three

HEIDELBERG DAYS: LOVE, FAITH, AND FAMILY

*"How good and pleasant it is when God's people
live together in unity."*
— Psalm 133:1 (NIV)

Before that fateful evening, our life in Heidelberg had been filled with warmth and purpose. The city, with its picturesque half-timbered houses and the stunning backdrop of the Neckar River, had become our cherished haven. Every cobblestone street we wandered echoed with the laughter of friends and the melodies of street musicians, weaving a vibrant tapestry of culture and community. Our days were rich with love and companionship. We often spent evenings gathering around the dinner table, sharing not just meals but stories that forged deeper connections. Faith was the cornerstone of our lives. Sundays were dedicated to church services at the historic St. Peter's Church, where the calming strains of hymns enveloped us, providing solace and a sense of belonging. Our home, a cozy three-bedroom apartment adorned with family photos and keepsakes from our travels, was always open to the African students studying at the University of Heidelberg. We welcomed them like family, creating a communal space filled with laughter and the aroma of traditional dishes like jollof rice and ugali. Those gatherings were not just meals; they were celebrations of our shared heritage, infusing our lives with hope and a sense of nostalgia.

I had a fulfilling job with the United States Army in the Housing department in Mannheim, a role that allowed me to contribute meaningfully while providing a stable life for my family. The work was challenging yet rewarding, and I took pride in helping military families find homes that suited their needs. With my brother and his family living nearby, our sons grew up immersed in love, learning invaluable life lessons from grandparents, aunts, and uncles who always enshrined the importance of togetherness. Life was easy, filled with playdates at the nearby park and trips to local festivals, and we felt safe, surrounded by a supportive network. But now, as I reflected on those cherished memories, those feelings of warmth and security seemed like a distant echo.

My brother Kofi introduced me to a vibrant Nigerian student named Ikunna during my visit to Heidelberg, and she eventually became an essential part of my wedding. Ikunna was a bright, bubbly young lady who was passionate about her studies in medicine at the prestigious University of Heidelberg. I first met her while I was living in London and visiting my brother Kofi in

Heidelberg; we instantly clicked. Her enthusiasm for life and her warm personality made it easy to forge a close friendship. When I got engaged and began planning my wedding, I knew I wanted Ikunna to be part of my big day, and it was a joy to ask her to be part of my bridal party. She made my special day happier and added a unique cultural view and joyful spirit to the celebration. Ikunna then introduced me to more African students also studying at the University of Heidelberg. Every Sunday after church, we would have a cultural evening at our home where I cooked Ghanaian foods, jollof rice, fried plantains, and savory meats for the students. We told stories about our countries and always had a great time.

Throughout the years, my home was a revolving door for students from all corners of the African continent. Each brought their flavor of life, their stories, and their dreams. Our home was transformed into a sanctuary, a place where students could find comfort and companionship. We supported them through exams, homesickness, and the challenges of living in a foreign land. We became a family, bound not by blood but by shared experiences and mutual respect. Our home was more than just a place to live; it was a vibrant haven filled with love, laughter, and a continual exchange of knowledge. The university students who came into our lives quickly became like big sisters and brothers to my sons, Kwame and Kwesi. Their willingness to help was unwavering; they babysat the boys whenever we needed to step out for errands or meetings, providing a warm and nurturing environment even in our absence. I recall the times when the students took Kwame to their university dorm. There, he was passed from one encouraging pair of hands to another, each student taking turns to engage him. They read stories aloud and spoke to him in German, ensuring he not only immersed himself in the language but also developed a love for learning.

My own journey of growth paralleled that of my children. Each interaction with the diverse group of students opened my eyes to new perspectives and cultures. I learned about their hopes, their dreams, and the challenges they faced, which deepened my empathy and broadened my worldview. My life grew richer in ways I had never anticipated, filling our home with creativity and curiosity.

This beautiful exchange of knowledge and love all began with my brother Kofi, who introduced me to Ikunna, who in turn, brought together a remarkable and diverse group of students whose presence transformed our family life and left an indelible mark on my heart.

Chapter Four

WHERE OUR STORY BEGAN

"True love is not about perfection; it is hidden in flaws,
found in grace, and built on choice."
—Unknown

O ur wedding day was a picture-perfect August day; the sun cast a gentle warmth while a soft breeze danced through the leafy branches of the trees surrounding the chapel. We deliberately chose this month for our special day, knowing that August in Heidelberg offers a unique charm. The lush green hills rolled gently in the background, their vibrant colors heightened by the summer sun, while the Neckar River shimmered like a ribbon of diamonds as it flowed gracefully through the heart of the city. The cobblestone streets, worn smooth by years of footsteps, buzzed with life—laughter and chatter mingling with the distant sound of a street musician's melody, creating an atmosphere of pure joy and celebration.

Family and friends had arrived from all corners of the world—Ghana, London, Canada, and New York—turning our wedding into an international reunion filled with love. We had planned every detail of the week meticulously, wanting our loved ones to experience the magic of this city we called home. Together, we wandered the halls of the Heidelberg Schloss, its ancient stones holding centuries of stories, and drifted along the Neckar River, the castle's reflection rippling in the water. Those moments brought our families closer, creating a connection that felt like it had always been there. The chapel was such a cozy and charming place, filled with beautiful fresh roses that made the whole room smell amazing. Soft music played, blending our cultures and making the vibe feel almost magical. We exchanged our vows with confidence, promising to be there for each other no matter what life threw our way. When we were announced as husband and wife, the cheers were loud and joyful, echoing off the chapel walls like a big celebration. The fun that followed was like a vibrant tapestry, mixing lively rhythms, heartfelt toasts full of love, and dancing that kept us going deep into the night.

In the months that followed, we settled into our new life together, cherishing the quiet moments of morning coffee, long walks through the Altstadt, and whispering dreams of the future. Then, something shifted. Mornings became heavier, my limbs sluggish, my stomach uneasy. At first, I brushed it off, but a lingering exhaustion told me something was different. A trip to the doctor confirmed what my heart had already begun to suspect: I was pregnant.

The news filled our home with a new kind of joy, one that ran deeper than any celebration we had known before. Tears brimmed in our eyes as we held each other, overwhelmed by the beautiful, terrifying, exhilarating journey that lay ahead. Our love had created a new life, and in that moment, everything felt just as it was meant to be. My pregnancy was a beautiful journey, full of moments of hope and excitement. My husband was by my side every step of the way, attending doctor's appointments and Lamaze classes with a dedication that made me feel supported and cherished. I immersed myself in Lamaze videos, determined to prepare myself for childbirth, carefully practicing the breathing techniques I saw. Each milestone in the pregnancy brought new excitement and anticipation, but one of the most memorable moments came during a routine doctor's visit. As the technician performed the ultrasound, we held our breath in anticipation. "It's a boy," the doctor announced, smiling warmly. Tears filled our eyes as we stared at the grainy black-and-white image of our son. He was healthy, and I was doing well, too, a blessing we didn't take for granted.

As my due date approached, the ladies at church organized a baby shower for me, filling the room with love, laughter, and an abundance of gifts for the baby. The atmosphere was warm and festive, a testament to the incredible community that surrounded us. Friends and family came together to celebrate this new chapter in our lives. Their encouragement and prayers strengthened my resolve for the journey ahead. One beautiful August morning, the moment we had been waiting for arrived. I went into labor. We had prepared meticulously for this day;

our suitcase was packed and ready by the door, filled with everything we thought we might need. My husband, ever calm and collected, helped me into the car, and we made our way to St. Elisabeth Krankenhaus. The hospital, with its peaceful atmosphere and caring staff, immediately put me at ease. A Catholic nun greeted us warmly at the entrance, her gentle demeanor comforting. She guided us to our room and helped us settle in.

The labor was long and exhausting, the hours blending in a haze of pain and determination. My husband and a midwife were by my side, holding my hand and encouraging me to breathe. As the sun began to rise, our beautiful baby boy, Kwame, entered the world. The moment I held him for the first time, an indescribable wave of love and wonder washed over me. His tiny fingers wrapped around mine, and I knew that life would never be the same. Bringing Kwame home was the start of a new adventure, one that was as challenging as it was rewarding. The sleepless nights, punctuated by the soft cries of a newborn, became my new reality. Diaper changes and feedings filled my days. Watching Kwame grow was nothing short of miraculous. His first smile melted my heart, his first laugh filled our home with joy, and his first steps were met with cheers and applause from us, the proud parents. Life took on a new rhythm, one centered around the needs and milestones of our son. We found joy in the simplest of moments: his fascination with a new toy, the way his face lit up when he recognized us. I would watch his tiny body nestling against mine as he slept. We embraced the journey of parenthood with open hearts and gratitude.

It was a privilege of working for the Department of Defense, which provided me with a unique perspective on international affairs. As a non-American citizen, I paid German taxes, an arrangement that came with its own set of benefits. One of the most noteworthy advantages was access to comprehensive German health insurance. This support allowed me the invaluable opportunity to take a couple of years of maternity leave, enabling me to fully embrace the joys of motherhood while ensuring my family's well-being.

Chapter Five

STILL UNDER ONE ROOF

"Even though I walk through the darkest valley,
I will fear no evil, for you are with me..."
— Psalm 23:4 (NIV)

After my husband asked for a divorce in front of our pastors, I felt as if the floor beneath me had collapsed. That conversation, though calm on the outside, shattered something deep within me. But what followed was even more confusing. Life continued, just with an ache that hovered like a low, persistent cloud. We didn't move out. We didn't even argue loudly or pack boxes. Instead, we quietly returned to the same house, the same kitchen, the same routines, but nothing was the same. Our home in Boxberg had always felt like a blessing. Nestled into a gentle slope, it had large glass windows that opened up to a view that could make you pause and take in the moment, no matter how hurried your day was. I loved standing in front of those windows in the early morning, tea in hand, watching fog roll through the valley and uncover Heidelberg's iconic red rooftops and church spires. It was our safe place, our dream realized.

We chose that home while I was pregnant with Kwame. We wanted a place that felt safe and full of promise. I imagined our children playing in the garden, riding bikes in the driveway, and growing up surrounded by peace and beauty. And for a time, that vision came to life. Kwame was my little explorer, always outdoors, digging holes with his plastic shovel, proudly declaring he had found dinosaur fossils. He loved learning the names of different dinosaurs and could tell anyone that a triceratops had three horns and a frill. The way he pronounced "paleontologist" made me laugh every time. That kind of dream, one I had never imagined for a child of mine, made me believe that maybe, just maybe, we had built something special.

Kwesi, in contrast, was gentler, more expressive with his hands and his voice. He would line up his Lego bricks by color, then create tiny cities to rule over. When he wasn't building, he was singing—soft gospel tunes he had picked up from our car rides or church services. His small fingers danced over his toy piano keys, and he sang as if the music lived inside him. Some days, he'd hum quietly while I cooked, unaware of how much comfort his presence brought me.

But once the divorce was out in the open, something invisible but undeniable shifted in our house. It was like a subtle but constant ache in the air, one that settled into the walls, into our silence, into our routines. The home that once rang with laughter and gospel music now echoed with silence. We never sat down to discuss how we'd move forward. We simply drifted into a strange pattern of cohabitation. We stopped sharing meals, stopped watching shows together, stopped touching, even in passing. Slowly and without words, we divided the house into emotional territories—his side, my side. He moved into the guest room, and I remained in the main bedroom. We shared a roof, but we lived in two different worlds.

The mornings became awkward ballets. I'd rise early, making breakfast for the boys, trying to keep my energy high for their sake. I'd hear him moving around, careful not to run into me. If we crossed paths in the kitchen, we offered brief nods or exchanged only necessary words. He usually took Kwame to kindergarten while I dropped Kwesi off at daycare, but the coordination felt cold and transactional. I missed the way we used to linger at the kitchen table, even after meals, sharing plans for the weekend or dreams for the future. I missed the music we used to play on Saturday mornings while cleaning the house. Now, the only sounds that filled the space were the boys playing or the distant hum of the dishwasher. Mealtimes became solo affairs. We no longer sat as a family. He would fix his plate and retreat to the guest room, and I would eat with the boys, putting on a brave face. We laughed about silly cartoons or their school stories, but underneath, there was an emptiness. They asked questions sometimes: "Why doesn't Daddy eat with us?" or "Can we watch a movie together like we used to?" I would answer as gently as I could, never placing blame, but always swallowing the pain.

Evenings used to be our time. After dinner, we'd gather in the living room, curled up with popcorn and fuzzy blankets, watching movies or talking about our week. Now, the living room felt abandoned. He stayed in the guest room; I stayed with the boys in the common areas, reading bedtime stories or letting them fall asleep beside me on the couch. Some nights, after they were in bed, I would walk quietly to the large window in the living room. I'd stare out at the glowing lights of Heidelberg, twinkling in the distance like tiny stars offering silent encouragement. I whispered Psalm 23:4 to myself more times than I could count. I carried it with me, when folding laundry, cooking dinner, and driving the boys to school. It became my anchor: "Even though I walk through the darkest valley, I will fear no evil, for you are with me…"

And I was walking through a valley. A long, dark, lonely valley where grief came in waves—not just the grief of a broken marriage, but of a fractured home. Of shared dreams that had turned into quiet strangers under the same roof. One night, after putting Kwame and Kwesi to bed, I returned to the kitchen to find a note he had left on the counter. Just a short message in his usual tidy handwriting: "I have to leave early tomorrow, so I won't be able to drop Kwame off. Can you handle both drop-offs?" I stared at it for a long time. It wasn't rude. It wasn't kind. It was practical, coldly so. I folded it and tucked it into a drawer. I don't know why, maybe because it was the only communication we had exchanged all day. Maybe because I was still holding on to a part of him. A part of us.

The boys, in their innocence, continued to bring joy into that heavy space. Kwame still dug up "fossils" and gave me updates on his latest findings. Kwesi continued to build and sing, sometimes stopping mid-song to say, "Mommy, listen!"

And I listened, oh, how I listened, because their joy reminded me that not everything was broken. Living under the same roof with someone who no longer wanted to walk life with you was a unique kind of pain. It was grief in slow motion. But in that pain, I learned how strong I was becoming. I learned how to protect my peace without pretending the pain didn't exist. I learned how to create a loving environment for my boys, even when my heart felt like it was breaking in two. And I prayed. Every day. Sometimes in whispers. Sometimes in sobs. I prayed that God would carry me through this valley. That He would heal what had been broken, even if that healing didn't come in the form of reconciliation. I prayed for clarity, for courage, and for comfort. I didn't know how or when I would heal. But I knew I would. I knew God was not finished with my story.

So I waited. I mothered. I prayed. I stood at the window. And I held on.

Chapter Six

ROOTED IN FAITH, BLOSSOMING IN LOVE

"She is clothed with strength and dignity;
she can laugh at the days to come."
— Proverbs 31:25 (NIV)

We attended an international church in Mannheim, Germany. The members from Germany, the United States, and various African countries brought a rich blend of cultures, languages, and traditions to the church. This diversity was reflected in the worship services, fellowship activities, and social gatherings. The church had a family atmosphere and a strong sense of community, where members felt like part of an extended family. This close-knit environment fostered strong bonds among members. As a church family, we supported one another in various ways, from practical help during difficult times to emotional and spiritual support. The church had regular social events, such as potlucks, cultural nights, and holiday celebrations, which allowed members to share their backgrounds and learn from one another. We participated in Bible studies and prayer groups that offered a more intimate setting for spiritual growth and fellowship and enhanced a sense of belonging. The church leadership reflected its diverse membership, with leaders from different backgrounds ensuring that all voices were heard and respected. We attended Bible studies on Wednesday evenings and church service on Sundays. We formed relationships with our church community that went beyond the church walls, creating lifelong friendships and a global support network.

Every year, our church organized a marriage retreat in the heart of the Black Forest in Baden-Württemberg. The retreat, a blend of serene nature and spiritual rejuvenation, was eagerly anticipated by couples. The Black Forest, with its dense trees, enchanting trails, and beautiful villages, provided the perfect backdrop for couples to reconnect and rediscover the essence of their union. The retreat's activities were a thoughtful mix of spiritual, emotional, and physical experiences. Mornings began with meditation and prayer sessions led by Pastor Sam. Afternoons were filled with guided hikes through the forest, encouraging couples to work together and communicate as they navigated the winding paths. On one such hike, we found ourselves at a beautiful, secluded lake. We sat by the water, holding hands and talking openly about our hopes and fears. Evenings were reserved for intimate dinners at the rustic lodge, where couples shared their stories and laughed over dinner. The lodge, adorned with twinkling fairy lights and fragrant flowers, felt like a magical haven. The highlight of the retreat was the renewal of vows ceremony held on the final day. Each couple reaffirmed their commitment to one another. Pastor Sam and Pat led the ceremony, their words resonating with sincerity and hope. Joy and love filled the couples' eyes as they held hands and repeated their vows together. Their voices blended beautifully.

During our first marriage retreat, I experienced a wave of emotions as a new mom leaving my son, Kwame, behind. The separation was especially tough for me, and it all came to a head on the first night of the retreat. I couldn't get in touch with the students who were looking after our son at our home, and I was overwhelmed with panic. I found myself in tears and seeking solace in the bathroom until one of my church sisters found me and offered reassurance. This was all before the time when cell phones were common, and the anxiety of not being able to reach them only added to my distress. It wasn't until a couple of hours later that the students finally called me back to explain that they had gone back to the dorm to retrieve some items.

A few weeks after returning home from the marriage retreat, I noticed subtle changes in my body, then nausea. These signs were familiar, reminiscent of my first pregnancy.

A mix of excitement and nervous anticipation filled my heart. I decided to find out. I like to be sure of anything before I tell anyone, so I took a pregnancy test and waited, each second feeling like an eternity. When the result appeared, a wave of emotions washed over me. "I am pregnant with my second child" I exclaimed. I shared the news with my husband when he got home from work. We were both happy that God had blessed us with a second child. Pregnancy the second time around was different. I was more aware of the journey ahead and more attuned to my needs and the baby's. There were challenges, of course; juggling the needs of a toddler while dealing with the physical demands of pregnancy was not easy. But we shared the responsibilities so that I could have enough rest. I had just returned to work from my maternity leave when I found out I was pregnant. I asked my supervisor if it was a problem for me to start another pregnancy journey while working and she told me that getting pregnant was not a crime. Whew! I felt happy and relieved to know I was supported at work.

Finally, the day arrived when I welcomed my second son into the world. My water broke around 7:30 p.m. We dropped off Kwame at a friend's house and headed to the hospital. I was in a lot of pain because the car shook while driving on the cobblestone streets. We arrived at the St. Elizabeth Krankenhaus, and I was wheeled into the labor room. The midwife swiftly and calmly took charge, instantly putting me at ease with her capable and reassuring approach. As my labor progressed, the persistent beeping of the monitor got on my nerves, and all I wanted was for it to be turned off. The midwife urgently summoned the doctor, signaling that it was time for me to push. Amidst the commotion, I could faintly make out their instructions for me to push. Mustering all my strength, I began to pray, pouring every ounce of effort into each push. Suddenly, the room erupted in jubilant shouts, and amidst it all, I heard the thunderous cry of my newborn baby. Kwesi, meaning "born on Sunday," felt like a precious gift, a blessing in every sense of the word. The nurses swiftly wrapped him in a soft blanket and placed him in my arms. His tiny fingers curled around mine, his eyes blinking as he took in his new surroundings. The moment I held him in my arms, I felt an overwhelming sense of completeness. Our family had grown, my heart had expanded, and I was ready for the beautiful chaos of life with two boys.

Life with my family was a whirlwind of activity, laughter, and a few tears. My two boys, Kwame and Kwesi, were bundles of energy and curiosity. Kwame, our eldest, was a curious child with an insatiable appetite for knowledge. He would spend time in the backyard digging for dinosaur bones. He believed he would one day be a paleontologist. Kwesi spent hours building intricate Lego structures, each one more complex than the last. I was blessed to stay home with the boys and teach them to read and learn about the world around them.

I found myself living a dream that many mothers cherish. Living in Heidelberg amidst the rich history and vibrant culture, I had the privilege of being a stay-at-home mom to my two wonderful boys. Our mornings began with the gentle chime of church bells from the church school up the hill where we lived. The boys and I would set out to explore the town's treasures. We often visited the Neckar River to feed the ducks and walk the Heidelberg Castle, where they would run freely in the sprawling gardens, their laughter echoing through the ancient walls. Being a stay-at-home mom allowed me to witness and cherish every milestone, from their first steps taken in our cozy living room to their enthusiastic attempts at speaking German with the local children. These are precious memories I still hold. We spent countless hours at the local parks, where the boys' imaginations soared as they played among the lush greenery and climbed the intricate playground structures.

One of the greatest blessings of our time in Heidelberg was the sense of community. Our neighbors quickly became friends, and their warmth and kindness made us feel at home. The boys thrived in this nurturing environment, forging friendships that transcended language barriers. The church women's group was a lifeline, offering support, advice, and companionship for me. We shared stories, recipes, and tips on navigating life in a foreign country, creating bonds that remain strong to this day. The boys and I would visit local markets, where the vibrant colors and enticing aromas of fresh produce captivated our senses. We attended festivals, embracing the traditions and customs that made Heidelberg so special. The boys learned to ride their bikes along the scenic paths, their confidence growing with each new skill mastered. These outdoor adventures not only fostered their physical development but also created a profound connection with nature. As the years passed, I watched my sons grow from curious toddlers to confident young boys, their hearts full of wonder and their minds eager to explore. Being a stay-at-home mom in Heidelberg was a gift, one that allowed me to nurture them, guide them, and be present for every precious moment. These experiences enriched Kwame and Kwesi's childhoods, instilling in them a deep appreciation for diversity and a love for learning.

Chapter Seven

WHEN THE WALLS CLOSED IN

"He heals the brokenhearted and binds up their wounds."
— Psalm 147:3 (NIV)

L iving in the same house after such a tumultuous shift was challenging. The boys were young, so we were able to play our game very well. We shielded them from the worst of our turmoil, keeping the routines steady: morning cuddles, after-school snacks, bedtime prayers. But behind those routines, the cracks were visible. The tension settled in the air like dust that refused to clear. There were fewer smiles between us, fewer words exchanged, and many nights spent in separate silence. As weeks turned into months, the initial shock gave way to a quieter, more reflective sadness. We stopped pretending that time alone would somehow make everything right. The conversations shifted from emotions to logistics—who would live where, how the custody would work, what we would tell the boys. They were too young to understand, but not too young to feel. I remember watching Kwame build his dinosaur world in the living room, narrating his little scientist stories with enthusiasm. Kwesi sang along to his toy piano while I stirred dinner on the stove. The normalcy of those moments both comforted and haunted me. Would these memories become tinged with sadness for them one day, just as they already were for me?

Then, one evening, the silence between my husband and me broke—shattered, really—during a heated argument in the kitchen. Our voices rose, words sharp and cutting, until exhaustion overtook the anger. And then came a kind of quiet we hadn't known before. Not the tense, stifled quiet we'd been living in, but the calm that follows surrender. We sat down and had the conversation that had been circling us for weeks. There was no more blame, just an aching honesty. The love that had once united us now felt like a weight—heavy and worn down by disappointments, misunderstandings, and broken trust. We both knew staying together for the sake of appearances would only deepen the wounds. The next day, I came home from work, turned the key in the door, and immediately sensed something different. The house felt lighter and quieter. He had moved out. His clothes were gone. The guest room, which had become his space, was bare. No note. No message. Just absence. And yet, the message was clear. This was final. A heavy silence blanketed the house that night as I prepared dinner alone. The boys asked where Daddy was. I swallowed the lump in my throat and said he was away on a work trip. It wasn't a lie, not exactly; it just wasn't the full truth. I needed more time. Time to think. Time to gather the courage to tell them what I hadn't even fully processed myself. But I decided to come up with a story so I wouldn't upset them.

Later that week, I reached out and asked if he would come by in the evenings to tuck them in, read their favorite bedtime stories, and keep that small part of their routine intact. To my surprise and gratitude, he agreed. Every evening, he rang the doorbell like a visitor, and the boys squealed in delight. Their giggles as he read *Foggy Goes to School* were the only sounds that made the house feel full again—if only for a little while. Those small mercies meant the world. But once the door closed behind him each night, the walls felt like they were closing in. I sat at the edge of my bed more nights than I can count, staring at nothing, willing my body to feel tired enough to rest. But sleep evaded me. My appetite disappeared. I lost weight without trying. Grief sat heavy on my chest, a constant, invisible burden I couldn't shake. I felt fragile, like I was holding everything together with frayed threads.

Still, I had to keep going. I had to be "Mommy." I had to sign permission slips, pack lunches, make pancakes, and hold bedtime together. My children needed me to show up, whole not fragmented. So I prayed, cried, and wrote in my journal. I listened to worship music that reminded me I wasn't alone. And slowly, in that sacred space between heartbreak and healing, I began to gain strength to take care of the boys.

Chapter Eight

THE PRAYER CLOSET

*"The Lord is close to the brokenhearted and saves
those who are crushed in spirit."*
— Psalm 34:18 (NIV)

Each night, after my sons were asleep and the last dish had been washed, I would retreat to the quiet of my walk-in closet. It was the only place in the house where I could breathe without pretense, where grief didn't need to be dressed up, and strength didn't have to be exhibited.

I'd sink to the floor, tears streaming down my face, and cry out to God. *Father, why am I going through this? I've tried to live a good life. I've been faithful, kind—even to those who have now turned against me. Why does it hurt so much?*

The closet became my sanctuary, a sacred space where the world's noise couldn't reach me. The soft hum of the overhead light, the scent of my sweaters above me, the gentle pull of the carpet beneath my knees, all of it wrapped around me like a quiet mercy. Here, I could be undone without fear. I could wail. I could whisper. I could worship.

I would sit with my Bible open, gripping it like a lifeline. Sometimes I read the words aloud in a trembling voice, sometimes in silence, letting the promises of Scripture seep into my brokenness like healing oil.

Some nights, the pain was so consuming, I sobbed until sleep overtook me. I would wake in the early hours of the morning, still curled on the closet floor, with a tear-stained Bible beneath my cheek and a dull ache in my chest. But one night was different. After hours of crying, praying, and begging God for peace, I drifted into sleep and woke up feeling... changed. Not fixed. Not whole. But lighter, like something had lifted.

I picked up my Bible and opened it to Psalm 91. I didn't choose the page, but my fingers simply landed there.

"He who dwells in the shelter of the Most High will rest in the shadow of the Almighty." I whispered the words into the darkness, my voice cracking. The idea of *resting* in God's shadow brought me unexpected comfort. I imagined myself like a child curling beneath a parent's arm, shielded from the storm. As I continued reading, the verses felt like they had been written just for me.

"He will cover you with his feathers, and under his wings, you will find refuge."

I closed my eyes and envisioned God like a great eagle, wings outstretched over me and my boys, protecting us from every hurt, shielding us from everything I couldn't control. The image stayed with me.

Night after night, I returned to that closet. Sometimes I knelt. Sometimes I lay flat on the floor, arms outstretched in surrender. I wept. I pleaded. I praised. I sat in silence. The Holy Spirit met me there, not in fireworks or voices from heaven, but in a steady presence that reminded me I wasn't alone.

Lord, I don't know how to do this. I don't know how to move forward, I prayed over and over. But always, Psalm 91 brought me back to peace.

"You will not fear the terror of night, nor the arrow that flies by day..."

"A thousand may fall at your side, ten thousand at your right hand, but it will not come near you..."

I traced the words with my fingertips like a promise written just for me. I began declaring those verses out loud, over myself, over my sons, over our future.

"For he will command his angels concerning you to guard you in all your ways."

That line became my anchor. I started praying it over their beds at night, whispering it into their rooms as they slept, asking God to send His angels to stand guard around them—body, mind, and soul. Over time, the prayer closet became more than a place of grief. It became a place of transformation. It was where fear met faith, where sorrow bowed to hope. It was holy ground, made sacred not by the space itself but by the presence that met me there. The prayers didn't change my past, but they changed me. They gave me the strength to get up the next morning. They gave me clarity to make wise choices. They reminded me that being a single mom didn't make me broken; it made me brave.

One morning, I woke up with resolve. I sat at my kitchen table with a cup of tea and made a list of people I could lean on, small steps I could take, and ways I could rebuild. I reminded myself that we would not be a sad story or a whispered cautionary tale. We would heal. The road ahead would not be easy, but I knew this: I would not walk it alone. Because I had found my hiding place. And there, in the shadow of the Almighty, I was learning how to rise again.

Chapter Nine

MAMA CAME,
AND SO DID GRACE

"Honor her for all that her hands have done, and let her works bring her praise at the city gate."
—Proverbs 31:31 (NIV)

I stared at my phone for what felt like hours, the screen aglow with my mother's name. The weight of what I had to share pressed so heavily on my chest, I could hardly breathe. Though the decision had been made for weeks now, saying it out loud—to her—would make it real in a way nothing else had.

Mama was in Ghana, thousands of miles away, but her presence had always felt near. Her voice was my comfort. Her faith was my anchor. I wasn't just worried about what she would say—I was worried about how my words would break the image she had of my "happily ever after."

With trembling fingers, I tapped her contact and hit the call button. One ring. Two. Three. I almost hung up. But just as I was about to, she answered.

"Vivian, my dear! How are you?" Her voice, bright and warm, washed over me like a balm.

"Hello, Mama," I replied, trying to keep my voice steady. "I'm okay. How are you?"

"Oh, you know me," she chuckled, "keeping busy with the usual. How is Germany? How is your husband?"

And there it was. That innocent question. My heart dropped.

"Mama," I said, "I need to talk to you about something important."

A pause. "What is it, Vivian? You sound worried."

I took a deep breath, the kind that gathers the strength of your ancestors.

"Mama, we're getting a divorce."

Silence.

I could hear the faint sounds of Accra in the background—children playing, vendors calling out, traffic humming—but her silence drowned it all out.

"Oh, Vivian," she finally said, her voice soft. "I'm so sorry to hear that. Are you all right?"

Tears welled in my eyes. "I'm getting there. It's been hard. I tried everything, Mama. I really did."

"I know you did," she whispered. "It must have been very difficult for both of you. I'm sorry you're going through this alone over there."

That's all it took. I broke. I poured it all out—the betrayal, the counseling, the aching silence, the sleepless nights. She didn't interrupt. She just listened. And when I was done, she said, "Life will test you, Vivian. But it's how you rise that matters. You are strong, my child. You will get through this."

Her words wrapped around me like a warm kente shawl. I could almost smell the shea butter in her hands as she blessed me through the line.

Then, almost without thinking, I asked, "Mama, can you come and stay with me and the boys?"

"Oh, Vivian," she said, her voice lighting up, "I've been waiting for you to ask. I would love nothing more than to be there for you and my grandchildren."

That conversation changed everything.

The day Mama arrived at Frankfurt Airport was the day everything shifted. I stood near the arrivals gate, my heart pounding, scanning every face. Then I saw her—dignified, radiant, dragging her suitcase like a woman on a mission. We embraced so tightly I didn't want to let go.

On the drive back to Heidelberg, she filled the car with stories about family, church, the woman selling waakye on our street, and her determination to help me get back on my feet. I told her everything—my fears, my doubts, my confusion. She didn't offer solutions. She offered herself.

When we pulled into the driveway, the boys ran out. "Grandma!" they screamed, rushing into her arms. For the first time in a long time, the house felt alive. The hallway rang with laughter, and the kitchen smelled like jollof and kelewele again.

She unpacked goodies from Accra—biscuits, chocolates, and little gifts—and the boys lit up with joy. That night, for the first time in months, I slept.

Over the following weeks, Mama became our rock. She cooked, cleaned, held Kwesi while he threw a tantrum, and laughed at Kwame's dinosaur facts. But more than that, she held *me*. We prayed together every morning and night, our voices soft but sure. She laid hands on me when I couldn't pray for myself and spoke life into places where hope had gone quiet.

One evening, after the boys were asleep, we sat in the living room watching a Nollywood drama and sipping tea. She reached over, held my hand, and said, "Vivian, life will keep testing you. But you, you are made of more. You are doing a wonderful job."

Her affirmation was healing.

The next day, I met with my husband at a small restaurant downtown to discuss custody and shared parenting. I had prepared myself to advocate for what I thought was fair—full custody, with visitation for him. But his words stopped me cold.

"The boys are American citizens," he said, "and I'm up for a PCS transfer back to the States. I'll be taking them with me."

Just like that.

He said a lawyer would contact me. I hadn't even *spoken* to a lawyer yet. I left the restaurant in a daze, my stomach tight with fear.

I drove straight to the park where Mama was with the boys. They were playing happily, unaware that their lives had just shifted beneath their feet.

I told her everything, my voice shaking.

"They can't take them from you," she said, her hands trembling as she held mine. "You're their mother."

"I know," I replied. "But I don't know German law. And I'm not American. What if..."

We sat in silence as the boys climbed into the car, laughing and yelling in the back seat. I looked at them through the rearview mirror and made a silent vow: *Whatever it takes, I will stay close to my children. I will not be separated from them.*

That night, I called my brother Kofi. I also spoke to his mother, Cora. I told them everything and asked for help navigating the legal system. I had no shame left, just purpose!

That week, I started making plans. If I had to move to the United States to fight for custody, then so be it. My story wouldn't end in fear. It would rise in *faith*.

Because now I was not walking alone! Mama came, and so did Grace.

Chapter Ten

THE STRENGTH BETWEEN US

"Though one may be overpowered, two can defend themselves.
A cord of three strands is not quickly broken."
—Ecclesiastes 4:12 (NIV)

Kofi and I had always shared a close bond, even though we didn't grow up in the same household. We were raised on different continents—he in Germany with his mother, Cora, and I in Accra with mine—but our hearts knew no distance. We were tied together not just by blood, but by a shared longing to know one another, and over the years, through visits and phone calls and deep conversations, we formed an unbreakable bond.

He was more than my brother. He was my confidant, my sounding board, and the person who could always make me laugh, even in my darkest moments. Whenever we spoke, we affectionately used our father's name before our own, a family tradition that carried weight and affection. He was "Yakpo Kofi," and I was "Yakpo Vivian." That naming reminded us of who we came from, and who we were to each other.

When my world began to unravel and the threat of separation turned into the reality of divorce, I knew I had to tell him. It wasn't just legal guidance I needed. I needed the grounding that came from hearing his voice.

I finally mustered the courage and called.

"Hey, Yakpo Vivian, how are you?" he answered, his voice warm and familiar, instantly putting me at ease.

I swallowed hard. "I'm okay, Yakpo Kofi," I replied softly, my voice fragile. "But there's something important I need to talk to you and Cora about. It's about the separation... and the divorce. I need help understanding German law."

There was a pause. I could almost hear the concern settle into his breath.

"Is everything okay?" he asked gently.

I nodded, though he couldn't see me. The silence spoke for me.

"No," I whispered, "I'm not okay. I'll tell you more when we meet."

"You don't have to go through this alone. We're here. Let's come over this weekend. Mama will be able to help you understand everything."

Relief flooded my chest. "Thank you, Kofi. That would mean so much."

Saturday came, and with it came comfort.

When the doorbell rang at noon, I opened it to see Kofi and Cora standing there, their faces wrapped in love and concern. My mother rushed forward, embracing Cora tightly. Though they had come from different places in my life, their arms shared the same mission—*protecting me*. Cora looked into my mother's eyes and said, "Don't worry. We're going to make sure she's okay."

I welcomed them in and offered something to drink. We settled in the living room, papers and documents stacked neatly beside me. I took a breath, gathered my strength, and began to speak.

I told them everything. The breakdown, the betrayal, the legal threat, the confusion. Cora listened with quiet empathy, her hands folded in her lap, her eyes never leaving mine.

When I finally stopped talking, she nodded. "In Germany, the laws are very clear about separation and divorce. The first step is a formal one-year separation. It's not just emotional distance, it's documented. Each of you must live separately and use that time to resolve issues related to children and finances."

Kofi leaned forward, his brow furrowed. "You'll want to keep records—texts, financial transactions, any agreements. It helps when you get to the official filing stage. And don't do this without legal help."

They both looked at me with such care, such quiet authority, I felt steadied.

Then Cora reached for her phone.

"I know someone," she said confidently. "A lawyer who specializes in family cases. I'll call her right now."

True to her word, she connected me with a woman named Frau Lizberg and even scheduled the appointment on my behalf. By the time they left that day, I felt stronger. Not because the problem had disappeared, but because I was no longer carrying it alone.

I met with Frau Lizberg a few days later. Her office was bright and tidy, her demeanor calm and welcoming. She greeted me with a warm smile and said in a low, gentle voice, "I've heard a bit about your case. You're not alone, and we're going to figure this out."

Her words wrapped around my heart like a prayer answered.

I sat across from her desk, clutching the folder of documents Cora helped me organize. She listened attentively as I shared my story. She asked questions that felt more like care than interrogation. When I finished, she nodded and explained my rights with patience and clarity.

"You have the right to custody, and we'll advocate for that," she said. "Because your boys are U.S. citizens, we may need to address relocation. That is a serious conversation—but not one you need to fear. You're their mother. We will protect that bond."

Tears blurred my vision.

"Thank you," I whispered.

"Vivian," she said, leaning forward with sincerity, "you're stronger than you know. And I'm honored to help you."

When I left her office, my heart was full of emotion, of fear, of hope. My marriage was dissolving, but something else was beginning to form: a new resolve. A fierce love. A deep conviction that my boys and I would make it. No matter what.

That day, I walked into work still feeling the sting of pain, but for the first time in a long while, I also felt something else: *protected.*

Chapter Eleven

WHEN THE SANCTUARY FELT LIKE A COURTROOM

"He heals the brokenhearted and binds up their wounds."
—Psalm 147:3 (NIV)

The first Sunday after the separation was the hardest. I woke up with a pit in my stomach, unsure if I should even go. But something in me, maybe the residue of routine or the stubborn hope that church would bring me peace, pushed me to get dressed, gather the boys, and drive to the same place we had attended as a family for years. Our church wasn't a traditional church building with stained-glass windows or steeples. It was a well-kept, modern building that had become our spiritual home over the years. The sanctuary had no pews, just rows of comfortable chairs arranged in neat lines, facing the stage where the praise and worship team led us into God's presence week after week. That morning, though, everything felt different.

As I drove into the parking lot, my hands shook a little on the steering wheel. I took a deep breath and got out of the car. My heels clicked on the pavement, creating a steady sound that helped calm my nerves. The boys walked ahead of me, unaware of the emotional storm brewing inside me. Their innocence was my anchor, and their smiles gave me temporary strength. But the moment I stepped into the building, the atmosphere shifted. The warmth I used to feel when being greeted with hugs and smiles was replaced by cautious nods and strained expressions. The sanctuary, once my refuge, now felt like a courtroom, and I, the defendant on trial. Every glance felt loaded. Every whisper felt like it was about me. I couldn't tell whether people were truly staring or if my own shame was warping my perception, but either way, I felt exposed. Naked. As if the pain of the separation was written all over me.

I took my usual seat near the middle, but it didn't feel like my seat anymore. The chair that once supported me now felt stiff and foreign. I kept my eyes on the stage, but my thoughts were anywhere but present. When the praise and worship team rose to lead the congregation, I mouthed the lyrics but couldn't feel the words. My voice, which once joined in full-throated praise, was stuck in my throat. I felt like an outsider in a place where I had once belonged. After service, I mustered the courage to speak with some of the leaders I respected. I hoped for comfort, for wisdom, for even a small dose of empathy. Instead, I was met with rehearsed responses: "Marriage is sacred." "You must fight for your family." "God hates divorce."

Yes, I knew those things. But where were the words that acknowledged the betrayal? The abuse of trust? The shattering of dreams?

I wasn't looking for permission to give up, I was looking for someone to see my pain and say, "God still loves you."

But that message never came. At least, not from them.

What came instead was an overwhelming sense of guilt. A guilt so thick it followed me home, crept into my prayers, and whispered to me late at night when the boys were asleep. I began to question everything: my faith, my value, my very place in the Kingdom of God. Sundays became unbearable. Every message about forgiveness felt like a veiled accusation. Every sermon about perseverance in marriage pierced like a blade. I sat silently, week after week, torn between wanting to be faithful to the routine of worship and wanting to disappear. To make matters worse, the church community began to fracture. Whispers spread. Some took sides. Some supported the other woman, which was painful, and others offered me words of encouragement and support. Those women of faith are still in my life. The hypocrisy cut deep. How could people who claimed to follow Christ ignore the truth of what had happened?

How could they sing of love and light while silently judging me in the shadows?

Still, God, in His faithfulness, always plants a remnant.

It began with a simple, heartfelt hug from one of my church sisters, Sheila, who had a genuine concern in her eyes. She enveloped me in warmth, whispered a prayer, and made it a point to check on me daily, offering her unwavering support. Shortly after, I received a thoughtful phone call from another sister, who gently asked if we could have a conversation. As time went on, God brought together a small group of women who supported me without needing answers or using tired phrases. They didn't ask for details or try to fix my problems. Instead, they sat with me in quiet comfort, offering their presence like a soothing balm. We prayed together, allowing our faith to keep us strong and allowing our tears to flow freely, showing our shared struggles and understanding. Each moment together felt like a special space where healing could start, based on real compassion and love. From this small group, something beautiful formed, a sisterhood built on shared brokenness, not perfection. We began meeting regularly. We shared our hearts over cups of tea and scriptures marked by tears. We prayed for each other's healing, encouraged each other's strength, and reminded each other that grace still surrounded us.

In that space, I began to find my footing again. I continued to journal my prayers, speaking declarations of truth over myself, even when I didn't feel them.

> "So do not fear, for I am with you; do not be dismayed, for I am your God."
>
> *—Isaiah 41:10*

It wasn't instant, and it wasn't easy. But over time, I realized that God had not abandoned me in that sanctuary. He was simply leading me out of the places that no longer fed my spirit into a deeper intimacy with Him. I had to reimagine what church meant to me. It was no longer about approval or fitting into a mold. It became about worshiping God for who He is, not for what people expected of me. I stopped seeking validation from the stage and found peace in God's presence. I stopped comparing my story to others and began to embrace the truth that my journey, though messy, was mine, and God was writing it with grace.

Divorce didn't make me less of a believer. It made me more aware of how desperately I needed grace. It didn't strip me of my faith; it deepened it. And I realized something profound: Christian guilt is loud, but God's grace is louder. The opinions of people may shake your confidence, but the Word of God will steady your soul. The church may falter, but God never does. And that is where I chose to rest.

Chapter Twelve

THE GAVEL AND THE CROSSROADS

*"The Lord is close to the brokenhearted and saves
those who are crushed in spirit."*
— Psalm 34:18 (NIV)

The air in the courtroom felt heavier than I had expected, thick with unspoken words, shattered dreams, and the weight of decisions that would shape the lives of two innocent boys. William and I sat on opposite sides, as distant in spirit as we were in physical space. Once, we had sat side by side, dreaming together about the future as a family. Now, all that remained between us was a long wooden table, a pair of lawyers, and the quiet ache of what could have been.

The room itself was sterile, with pale walls, high windows letting in cold daylight, and the faint echo of footsteps on polished floors. Yet to me, it felt like the walls were closing in.

The polished wood of the judge's bench gleamed under the overhead lights, but there was no warmth in this place, only the clinical process of untangling lives. I glanced briefly at William. His face was a mask of composure, but I knew him well enough to see the storm behind his eyes. We were both exhausted, not just from the long hours spent in legal discussions, but from the emotional toll of watching our family fracture piece by piece.

At the center of it all were Kwame and Kwesi, our beautiful boys. They were too young to understand why Mommy's smile didn't quite reach her eyes these days, or why Daddy wasn't always home anymore. Their laughter still filled the corners of my heart, reminding me daily of what I was fighting for.

Frau Lizberg, my lawyer, adjusted her glasses and stood confidently. A pillar of calm in the chaos, she spoke with a grace that steadied my nerves.

"Your Honor," she began, her voice firm but respectful, "my client, Mrs. Newton, has been the anchor in her sons' lives. She has nurtured them, provided stability, and ensured their emotional and physical well-being throughout this difficult time."

I sat up straighter, clutching the small pendant around my neck, a gift from Mama, engraved with a simple cross. A silent prayer passed through my lips: *Lord, give me strength.*

William's lawyer rose next, sharp like a blade, every word calculated. "Your Honor, my client is not merely a visitor in his children's lives. He has been present, engaged, and loving. This is not a case of abandonment or neglect. It is about preserving a father's rightful place."

The judge, a man with graying hair and weary eyes that had likely seen too many broken families, listened intently. When it was my turn, my heart pounded so loudly I feared it would drown out my words. But when I stood, a calmness washed over me, not from within, but from above.

"Your Honor," I began, my voice steady despite the lump in my throat, "Kwame and Kwesi are my heart. Every decision I've made, every sacrifice, has been for them. They need more than love. They need consistency, a sense of home. I can give them that. I have always given them that."

Then came William's voice, steady but laced with something that sounded almost like regret. "I love my sons," he said, his gaze fixed on the judge, avoiding mine. "Vivian is a wonderful mother, but we are both moving to the United States, just to different states. I believe shared custody is best."

Silence followed, heavy, suffocating silence, as the judge leaned back in his chair, fingers steepled in thought. The ticking of the courtroom clock suddenly became the loudest sound in the room.

Finally, he spoke.

"This is not an easy decision. It's clear both parents love their children deeply." His eyes shifted to me. "Vivian, have you decided which state you will move to?"

I shook my head slightly. "Not yet, Your Honor. Our family is in New York, but nothing is confirmed."

He turned to William. "And you?"

"I will be relocating to Virginia, Your Honor."

The judge nodded solemnly before delivering his verdict. "In the best interest of Kwame and Kwesi, I am granting joint custody."

He leaned forward, his voice firm but empathetic. "Given that both parents will reside in different states, William will have structured visitation rights during school holidays, summer vacations, alternating Christmases, and spring breaks. Both parents must coordinate travel and ensure the boys maintain strong relationships with both of you."

When the judge finally set down his papers, he looked at us both with a weariness that only comes from years of witnessing families unravel before his bench.

"This is not about either parent winning," he said. "This is about two young boys who deserve to know they are loved by both their mother and their father, no matter how many miles lie between you."

And just like that, the gavel came down with a dull thud, sealing our fate.

Chapter Thirteen

A BIRTHDAY IN THE SHADOW OF TRAGEDY

"God is our refuge and strength, an ever-present help in trouble.
Therefore, we will not fear, though the earth give way."
— Psalm 46:1-2 (NIV)

The afternoon air in Heidelberg felt crisp, the kind of early autumn coolness that hinted at the changing season. It was my birthday, but the day carried a heaviness I couldn't shake. The weight of my impending divorce pressed down on me, a dull ache in the background of my thoughts. Even so, my friends had insisted on taking me out to dinner that evening. "You need this," they had said. And maybe they were right. Maybe, for one night, I could forget about the upheaval in my life and just celebrate, if only for a few hours. As I wrapped up my workday, I noticed a shift in the air. Colleagues were whispering, their faces drawn, their movements sharp with urgency. Small clusters of people had formed around televisions in the break room and offices. I caught snippets of conversation, something about a plane crash in New York. A terrible accident, I assumed.

I had no reason to linger. My thoughts were fixed on getting home, changing, and preparing for the evening ahead. So, I walked past them, oblivious to the magnitude of what was unfolding. It wasn't until I stepped into our home, kicked off my shoes, and absentmindedly turned on the television that reality slammed into me. The second plane had just struck the South Tower. The image on the screen didn't seem real. A gaping fireball, thick black smoke swallowing the sky. A city in chaos. People were running, screaming, and covered in dust. My breath caught in my throat. This wasn't an accident. This was something else, something unthinkable. Time slowed, my body frozen in place. My mind raced to New York, to the place my in-laws lived. To the place my boys and I might soon be moving. To the countless people inside those towers. The weight of it all pressed against my chest.

The phone rang, jolting me back to the present. It was one of my friends. "Are we still going out?" she asked, her voice hesitant, uncertain. The question felt surreal. How could I celebrate when the world had just been torn apart? But at the same time, what else was there to do? Sitting alone, watching horror unfold on the screen, wouldn't change anything. Maybe, just maybe, being with people who cared about me, who reminded me that life still moved forward, would help. So, I said yes.

I didn't know then that the world had just changed forever, that everything—my life, my future, my understanding of security—had shifted in a single, shattering moment. But that night, amid the chaos, I chose to hold on to the one thing I still had: the people around me. The drive to the restaurant was eerily quiet. Usually, my friends and I filled car rides with laughter and conversation, but that night, silence wrapped around us like a heavy fog. The events of the day hung in the air, unspoken yet undeniably present. Even the streets of Heidelberg felt different, subdued, tense, as if the city itself was holding its breath. When we arrived at the restaurant, the usual warmth of the place felt muted. People spoke in hushed tones, their eyes darting toward the televisions mounted in the corners. The news played on a loop, replaying the devastation in New York, the Pentagon, and Pennsylvania. It was as if the world had stopped spinning, caught in an endless reel of horror and disbelief.

We slid into our seats, exchanging small smiles of reassurance, but there was no mistaking the unease settling over us. The server approached, her expression kind yet distant, as if she too was struggling to process the weight of the day. We picked up the menus, but our minds weren't on food. Before we could even place our orders, one of my friends' phones buzzed. She answered, and her face went pale. "My husband just called," she said, her voice barely above a whisper. "There's a curfew in place. All Americans working for the Department of Defense must be home immediately."

The words sent a fresh wave of anxiety through me. I hadn't even considered that there could be more threats, that the attacks in the U.S. could have repercussions for those of us living abroad. The uncertainty of it all was unnerving. We looked at each other, silently acknowledging what had to be done. The dinner would have to wait. I caught the server's eye, offering a small apologetic nod as we stood. She simply nodded back, as if she had expected this.

As we stepped outside, the night air felt unnaturally still. The usual hum of the city had dulled, replaced by an uneasy quiet. The drive back home felt much shorter than the one to the restaurant, as if time had collapsed in on itself. My birthday, once meant to be a moment of joy, had been swallowed by something much larger than myself. When I walked through the door of our home, my mother was exactly where I had left her, on the couch, her eyes glued to CNN. The screen flickered with images of the Twin Towers engulfed in flames, bodies running, smoke billowing. The same footage, over and over again.

"Please, Mama," I said, my voice barely above a whisper. "Turn it off."

She looked up at me, her eyes filled with sadness. Her hand hovered over the remote, hesitating. I knew she wanted to stay informed, to make sense of what had happened. But I couldn't take another second of it. I had been calling my sister-in-law and mother-in-law all evening, desperate to hear their voices, but there had been nothing. No answer. No reassurance. Just silence.

"I can't reach them," I admitted, sinking onto the couch beside her. My voice cracked. "It's causing me anxiety."

She nodded slowly and clicked off the television. The silence that followed was deafening. For the first time that day, there was no background noise, no news anchors narrating the nightmare. It was just me and my mother, and we felt the pressure of the unknown around us.

I reached for her hand. "Let's pray," I whispered, my throat tight. She gave my fingers a gentle squeeze, and together, we bowed our heads. I let the words spill out: prayers for my in-laws, for the families who had lost loved ones, for the rescue workers, for the world that had just changed in an instant. As I spoke, the fear clawing at my insides loosened, just a little. I felt the warmth of my mother's presence beside me, her steady murmurs of faith anchoring me.

"It's going to be okay," she whispered as I wiped away a tear. I wanted to believe her.

The next morning, my phone rang, jolting me from a restless sleep. My heart pounded as I grabbed it.

"Sister-in-law," the caller ID read, "Auntie Judy."

My hands trembled as I answered. "Hello?"

Her voice was rushed but steady. "We're okay. Ma is okay. We're all safe."

The breath I had been holding in for what felt like an eternity finally escaped. Relief flooded through me, a tidal wave washing away the worst of my fears. I whispered a thank you to God, my chest finally loosening.

I called out to my Mama. "They're safe; Auntie Judy and the family in New York are safe," I said, exhaling.

She responded, "Hallelujah, thank you, Lord."

But the relief was fleeting. Outside, the world was still holding its breath. School and work were canceled. Military families were told to stay home. The city felt different, quieter, heavier. The days that followed were slow, surreal, filled with uncertainty. Eventually, life resumed, but nothing would ever be the same again. The world had changed. I had changed.

Chapter Fourteen

A BITTERSWEET GOODBYE
AND A BIRTHDAY BLESSING

"For I know the plans I have for you," declares the Lord,
"plans to prosper you and not to harm you,
plans to give you hope and a future."
—Jeremiah 29:11 (NIV)

As mama prepared to return to Ghana, she made sure to thank my sister-in-law and her husband for all their help and kindness. The day we took her to the airport was filled with mixed emotions. We hugged her tightly, tears rolling down our cheeks, and said heartfelt prayers for a safe journey. Watching her walk through the airport doors made us feel the reality of her departure, and the boys kept waving until she disappeared from sight.

After mama left, my sister-in-law, Auntie Judy, kindly offered to fly back to help me with the packing. Her support meant a lot to me during this busy and emotional time. The days before the move passed by in a blur. I spent hours sorting through our belongings, deciding what to keep, what to give away, and what to pack for our journey. Each item held a memory, making the process even more overwhelming. The night before our flight to New York, our friends came over to say goodbye. There were lots of hugs, tears, and words of encouragement. Our neighbors also stopped by, expressing how much they would miss the boys. They had grown fond of the children, often surprising them with warm cookies or cakes fresh from the oven. The boys were excited about the move but also sad about leaving their home in Boxberg. I reassured them, saying, "This is going to be an amazing adventure. We will make new friends, discover new places, and create wonderful memories together."

Finally, the morning of August 27, 2002, arrived. We loaded our suitcases into the car and left Heidelberg, heading to Frankfurt Airport. My heart raced as we pulled up to the terminal, the reality of our big move hitting me all at once. We checked in at the Lufthansa kiosk, where the attendant gave me a puzzled look while staring at her screen. She whispered something to a colleague, and then they both turned to me.

"There seems to be a seating issue," the man explained. "We don't have seats together. Please wait until all the passengers have boarded."

I was shocked. *How did I miss checking our seats?* I wondered, my stomach tightening with worry. The boys and I found a place to sit and waited anxiously. When the plane was almost full, the man returned and said, "Please follow me."

We walked through the jet bridge and into the plane. As we entered, I noticed him turning left. I hesitated, thinking, *That's not the way to the economy section.* Before I could say anything, he leaned in and whispered, "We couldn't find seats together, so we've upgraded you to Business Class. Enjoy your flight." "Thank you so much!" I said, my face lighting up. On the inside, I was doing a happy dance. The boys' eyes widened in amazement as we settled into the wide, comfortable seats. The journey to our new life had just gotten a little sweeter.

As our plane soared into the sky, I looked out of the window, marveling at the sight of the city gradually shrinking into a mere speck in the distance, a fleeting memory of the world we were leaving behind. Our journey was smooth and comfortable, and as luck would have it, it was Kwame's birthday. To our delighted surprise, the airline staff presented him with a beautifully curated gift basket. To make the day even more memorable, the flight attendants came together to serenade him with a heartfelt rendition of "Happy Birthday." In that beautiful moment, emotions overwhelmed me, and it seemed as if a divine reassurance was being whispered to me, promising that everything would be all right for me and my boys.

Chapter Fifteen

A NEW BEGINNING IN BROOKLYN

*"Be strong and courageous. Do not be afraid;
do not be discouraged, for the Lord your God
will be with you wherever you go."*
— Joshua 1:9 (NIV)

The pilot's voice crackled over the intercom, his German accent distinct and authoritative. "Ladies and gentlemen, we have begun our descent into JFK International Airport. Please turn off all portable electronic devices until we have arrived at the gate. Ensure your seat backs are in the upright position, tray tables are stowed, and seat belts are securely fastened. We anticipate landing shortly. Thank you for flying with Lufthansa, and welcome to New York."

As the plane passed through thick clouds, the New York City skyline appeared, glowing in the soft orange light of the sunset. My heart raced with a cocktail of emotions: fear, hope, and the sheer weight of the unknown. This was it. A new chapter, a new country, a new identity: single mother to two little boys navigating life in Brooklyn, New York.

The wheels screeched against the runway, and the plane slowed to a crawl. My sons, Kwesi and Kwame, stirred beside me. "Are we here, Mama?" Kwesi asked, rubbing his eyes. "Yes, sweetheart," I whispered, forcing a smile. "We're home." After the tedious shuffle through immigration and baggage claim, we emerged into the terminal, where a sharp gust of air from the automatic doors greeted us like a cold slap. Outside, the driver my sister-in-law, Auntie Judy, had arranged was waiting, holding a sign with my name in bold black letters. He offered a polite nod as he helped with our luggage.

"Welcome to New York," he said.

The boys pressed their noses against the car windows as we drove across the Brooklyn Bridge. The thick steel cables stretched high above us, crisscrossing like a giant web. Beyond the cables, the city spread out in every direction. Tall buildings stood like quiet giants, their windows glowing with hundreds of tiny lights, like stars scattered across the night sky. Down below, the streets were busy and full of energy. Yellow taxis zipped past, their horns beeping loudly. Street vendors stood by their carts, calling out to people passing by, offering hot pretzels, roasted peanuts, and steaming hot dogs. Pedestrians moved quickly along the sidewalks, their footsteps blending with the city's endless hum. The boys watched everything in amazement, their eyes wide with wonder.

"Mom, look!" Kwame pointed to a vibrant mural on a building's side, a kaleidoscope of colors depicting a family holding hands.

"Beautiful, isn't it?" I said, my voice thick with emotion. The mural felt like a whisper of encouragement, a silent reminder that we, too, were a family starting anew.

Brooklyn was a world away from the cobblestone streets and peaceful charm of Heidelberg. Here, everything seemed louder, faster, more intense. As we turned into a quiet, tree-lined street in Park Slope, the frenetic energy gave way to a more familiar calm. Brownstones stood shoulder to shoulder like old friends, their stoops adorned with pumpkins and wreaths hinting at the holiday season.

Auntie Judy and Uncle Richie lived in a spacious apartment on the top floor of a red-brick building. Inside, the apartment was warm and inviting. The living room was filled with the scent of cinnamon and vanilla. Auntie Judy led us down the hall to our rooms: a cozy space with bunk beds for the boys, a colorful world map on the wall, and a small desk stocked with crayons and pencils. "Thank you, Auntie Judy," I said.

Later that night, as the boys drifted into exhausted sleep, I sat by the window gazing out at the city lights. The enormity of the journey hit me like a wave. My marriage was over. I was now both mother and father, guide and protector. My mother-in-law, who lived a few blocks down from us, had prayed for reconciliation and hoped and wished for her son to do the right thing, but I knew that chapter had ended long before I boarded the plane in Germany.

Tears pricked my eyes, but I didn't let them fall. Tomorrow, I would find my footing. Tomorrow, I would begin again.

Brooklyn, with all its noise and promise, would become our home. I whispered into the quiet night, "We made it."

That first night, after the boys had finally settled down and gone to sleep, I sat with Auntie Judy and Uncle Richie in the living room. They talked about the logistics of the move, the challenges ahead, and the support they could offer. "Take your time," Uncle Richie said. "We're here for you. There's no rush to find your place. Focus on settling in and finding a job first." I expressed my gratitude to them and retired to bed. It's amazing how unpredictable life can be. As I lay in bed, in a new country, preparing to embark on a new chapter of my life, I found myself reflecting on the day's events. "Father God, I thank you for keeping us safe," I whispered my prayers before drifting off to sleep.

The next morning, I woke up to the sound of sirens and car horns. The noise was loud but full of life. Brooklyn was alive, a place where people from all over the world came together. Over the next few weeks, we started to settle into our new life. It wasn't easy, but little by little, we found our way. I spent my days exploring the neighborhood with Kwame and Kwesi. We stopped at fruit stands to buy mangoes, the sweet smell reminding me of home. No matter where I've lived, whether in London, Heidelberg or now Brooklyn, I've always found a way to feel at home. We found parks where the boys could run and play. We discovered libraries where they could get lost in books, so their imaginations could take them to faraway places. But Brooklyn was fast! Everyone seemed to be in a hurry, always moving, always busy. At first, it was hard to keep up. The city felt overwhelming, like it never stopped. But I was determined to make it work. This was our new home, and I wanted to find our place in it. Brooklyn was challenging, but it was also full of life, and we were ready to embrace it.

Our first few weeks were a whirlwind of activities. Weekends in Brooklyn were delightful. Saturday mornings started with a visit to the Greenmarket. The market was a sensory overload in the best way possible, filled with fresh produce, artisanal bread, and flowers. We'd often grab a juice from one of the local vendors and stroll through the market, picking up ingredients for our weekend meals. Some afternoons we visited the Brooklyn Museum or the Botanic Garden, both offering a perfect blend of culture and nature. We went to Chinatown most Saturday evenings for dinner. We also discovered a plethora of restaurants offering cuisines from all over the world. From authentic Italian pizzas to spicy Thai curries, our taste buds were constantly on an adventure.

Finding a church where we could worship together as a family was deeply important to me. After some searching, we discovered the Christian Culture Center (CCC) in Brooklyn. From the moment we stepped through its doors, we felt a sense of belonging. The sanctuary was vast and inviting, with high ceilings that seemed to stretch toward heaven and large windows that covered the room in soft, natural light. The warm, golden tones of the woodwork created a comforting atmosphere.

On Sunday mornings, I would pick up my mother-in-law, and together, with the boys in tow, we'd make our way to the church. We usually sat on the balcony, where the boys could get a clear view of the stage. From that vantage point, they could see everything: the musicians, the singers, and the pastor who stood at the front, often writing key points on a board to make his lessons more tangible. Kwame, always curious and attentive, took diligent notes, his small hand moving quickly across the pages of his notebook. The praise and worship team always filled the sanctuary with uplifting music. Their voices blended beautifully, creating a sound that felt like it reached the heavens. They usually sang familiar hymns and modern songs. The congregation would join in, and soon the whole sanctuary would be singing in praise.

When I began looking for the right school for my seven-year-old son, Kwame, I quickly learned that public schools in the United States have specific rules about where children can go to school. These rules are based on the neighborhood you live in, which is called district zoning. After checking the zoning rules for our area, I found out that our assigned public school was PS 312. I decided to visit the school to see if it would be a good fit for Kwame. The staff was welcoming, and the classrooms looked well-organized and engaging. After our visit, we completed the necessary paperwork, and Kwame was officially registered to start second grade.

The first day of school was filled with excitement. As we prepared to leave the house that morning, Kwame was ready with his backpack, full of anticipation. His younger brother, Kwesi, also grabbed his small backpack and eagerly joined us. He assumed that he, too, would be starting school that day. However, when we arrived at PS 312 and he realized that he wasn't going to school with his big brother, he burst into tears. It was heartbreaking to see him so disappointed. I hugged him, wiped his tears, and gently promised that I would find a daycare for him soon.

On our walk back home, I noticed a group of children, some about Kwesi's age, holding hands with adults as they walked into a nearby Jewish temple. This caught my attention, so the next day, after dropping Kwame off at school, I decided to stop by the temple to ask about the children I had seen. To my surprise, I discovered that the temple Shalom operated a preschool program. It was conveniently located just a few blocks from PS 312, which made it an ideal option for us. I filled out the application forms, and soon, Kwesi was enrolled in the preschool.

Even though both boys were now settled in school, I felt compelled to explore more educational opportunities for them. I heard about a private school fair taking place in Manhattan and decided to attend. The event featured several well-known private schools, each with a booth and representatives who were eager to share information about their programs. I went from table to table, collecting brochures, asking questions, and learning about the admissions process.

When I got home, I couldn't stop thinking about the possibilities. The idea of my children attending a prestigious private school was exciting. I imagined them benefiting from smaller class sizes, more resources, and unique learning experiences. I decided to apply to a few schools, and after completing the applications and scheduling placement tests, we received good news: both boys were accepted to several of the schools we had applied to. Despite the excitement, however, reality quickly set in. The tuition for these private schools was very high, and as much as I wanted the best for my children, I had to consider our financial situation. After much thought, I made the practical decision to keep Kwame at PS 312 and leave Kwesi at the Jewish daycare center.

While managing the boys' education, I was also dealing with the emotional and legal challenges of my divorce, which was still ongoing in Germany. The stress was overwhelming at times, and I often wondered if it would be better to move back to Europe, where I had family, friends, and a familiar work environment. The thought of returning to a known place was comforting, but it also meant uprooting the boys again and starting over. I wrestled with these thoughts for weeks. Ultimately, I realized that building a stable life in the United States was the best decision for my family. It was a leap into the unknown, but I knew that embracing this new chapter sooner rather than later would help us create the stable, fulfilling life I envisioned for my boys and myself.

Chapter Sixteen

WHEN ENDINGS LEAD TO NEW BEGINNINGS

"The Lord is close to the brokenhearted and saves those who are crushed in spirit."
— Psalm 34:18 (NIV)

The phone rang, and as I picked up the phone, the familiar German accent of my lawyer greeted me. Her tone was practical and professional, yet somehow softened, as though she knew this news would settle heavily. "It's official," she said simply. "The divorce is finalized. You're now legally divorced." The words echoed for a moment, lingering in the air like a faint chime, marking the end of an era. In an instant, my life, once shared, had been neatly divided, documented, and signed away. I was left standing on the precipice of something new, unsteady, yet undeniably my own. I thanked her and we ended the call. After the phone call,

I found myself sitting on the cold stone stairs, almost unaware of the world around me. The weight of the moment felt heavy and suffocating, as if gravity itself was working against me. I thought I would be prepared for this, that it would not be too bad. But instead, a wave of sadness hit me, overwhelming and fierce, like a tidal wave pulling me under.

I began to sob uncontrollably. Each cry was deep and raw, coming from a hidden place inside me, a well of grief I had never touched before. Tears streamed down my face, each one carrying bits of dreams, cherished memories, and plans that would never happen. I wasn't just mourning the end of my marriage; I was grieving for the woman I used to be and the hopes I had for a future that now felt shattered. Sitting on those hard stairs, I felt a part of me fall apart, leaving behind an emptiness that was both painful and unfinished.

After picking the boys up, I decided we'd go for lunch at their favorite spot, a little restaurant that always brought smiles to their faces. They chattered excitedly from the back seat, their voices filled with the kind of energy only children seem to have after school, and I felt the weight of my earlier sorrow lift, if only a little. When we arrived, they practically ran inside the restaurant, each one knowing exactly what they wanted to order.

Watching them brought me pure joy. As they enjoyed their meals, I couldn't help but smile. I felt warmth fill my heart. Surrounded by the laughter and ease of my boys, I realized that despite my losses, I still had them. They were my reasons to keep moving forward.

A week after my divorce was finalized, I was trying to adjust to my new reality when my phone rang. It was Cora, my brother

Kofi's mother, calling from Germany. Her voice trembled as she delivered the devastating news: my father had passed away on a flight en route to Accra from London. The words echoed in my mind, refusing to settle into reality. My father and I had just spoken a few weeks earlier. He had been in high spirits, telling me he would be in New York soon, and we had planned to meet to discuss my next steps in life. That conversation now felt like a painfully severed thread in the fabric of my life, leaving a gap that I couldn't help but mourn.

Overwhelmed with grief, I somehow managed to call my mother. She picked up the phone, and I burst into tears before I could say a word. Her voice cracked as she admitted she had been dreading calling me. She was afraid the news would be too much for me to bear after the emotional toll of my divorce. She comforted me and prayed with me, asking God to give me peace. After composing myself, I called Kofi. It was a difficult conversation, filled with long silences punctuated by shared memories of the last time we saw our father in Ghana. We discussed the next steps: how we would arrange to travel to Ghana for the funeral and reconnect with our uncles and extended family to plan the ceremonies. The days that followed were a whirlwind of logistics and grief. I found myself grappling with a mix of emotions: sorrow for the loss of my father, guilt for not being closer during his final moments, and anxiety about returning to Ghana after so many years away. My father was a deeply respected man in our family and community. I knew his funeral would be a monumental event, filled with traditions, rituals, and people who would want to honor his life.

In the second week of December, I prepared for a journey I had never wanted to take: traveling to Ghana for my father's funeral. My heart was heavy, knowing I would leave my boys behind, but my Auntie Judy kindly offered to care for them while I was away. The nine-hour flight from JFK to Accra felt like an eternity. Sleep eluded me, and my thoughts swirled with memories of the last time I saw my dad and the reality of saying goodbye. When the plane landed in Accra in the early morning, the familiar humid air and the sight of my family waiting for me brought both comfort and sorrow. As I stepped into their embrace, the weight of our collective grief broke through, and tears flowed freely. The drive to my mother's house was unusually quiet. The roads seemed unfamiliar in my haze of emotions, and every mile felt like an eternity. When we finally arrived, my mother's face mirrored the pain in my heart. There were no words, just the shared understanding of loss.

The next day, my brother Kofi arrived. Meeting him at the airport was bittersweet; we hadn't seen each other in some time, and now we were reunited under the shadow of our father's passing. As we hugged, tears came easily. The funeral itself was a profound and beautiful tribute to my father's life. Held in our hometown, it was filled with prayers, songs, and stories that captured the essence of the man we loved. When the burial was over, I felt the pull of another responsibility: returning to my boys. On Christmas Eve, I boarded a plane back to New York, determined to be with them for the holiday. Stepping outside the terminal, I saw my boys and Auntie Judy waiting. The boys ran to me, and I hugged them tightly.

Christmas in New York City was pure magic. The streets sparkled with lights and decorations, transforming the bustling city into a winter wonderland. Bundled up against the chill, we wandered through the festive crowds, each street seeming more enchanting than the last. The boys' eyes were wide with excitement as they took it all in, pointing out every wreath, every tree, every flickering light that lined the sidewalks. The highlight was seeing the Rockettes at Radio City. The boys were captivated, leaning forward in their seats, dazzled by the lights, the music, and the flawless high kicks that seemed to defy gravity. I watched their faces, lit with amazement, and felt joy that God was keeping us even though we were in our valley days.

Chapter Seventeen

A LEAP OF FAITH

"Trust in the Lord with all your heart and lean not on your own understanding; in all your ways submit to Him, and He will make your paths straight."
— Proverbs 3:5-6 (NIV)

In the absence of formal therapy, I found ways to cope or at least, I tried to. I began writing inspirations daily and emailing them to friends. It became a small, purposeful ritual, a way to remind myself that even amid my struggles, I still had something to offer. Writing those inspirations didn't just help me; it connected me to others, forming a fragile but meaningful thread to the world outside my sadness. Church and Bible study became my sanctuary. I threw myself into the teachings, clinging to them as lifelines. I wasn't just seeking God; I was searching for meaning, for answers, for a glimmer of hope that my life could one day feel full again. The community I found there helped to buoy me, their prayers and encouragement forming a patchwork of support. But the truth was I was still carrying so much inside that I wasn't ready to face yet. Therapy wasn't an option for me then, not because I didn't need it, but because I didn't know how to ask for it. Instead, I relied on long phone conversations with friends. We would talk for hours, sharing stories, laughter, and tears. They probably didn't know it, but those conversations were my therapy. They were the spaces where I felt seen and heard, even when I couldn't fully understand myself. Brooklyn was a place of contrast for me. It was where I began to piece together a new life, even as I felt like I was falling apart. It was where I learned to keep going, even when I didn't know how. And it was where I began to discover, little by little, that sadness is not the end of the story.

Living with my sister-in-law and her husband in New York was a blessing in so many ways. Their home was warm and inviting, a refuge in a time of uncertainty. They welcomed the boys and me with open arms, offering a safe place to land when we needed it the most. For the first time in what felt like forever, I could breathe. I didn't have to worry about where we would sleep or if there would be food on the table. The boys had a stable routine, and I had a moment to catch my breath. But as comforting as their generosity was, I began to feel the pull toward independence. I wanted my own space, a place where I could rebuild my life, create new memories, and start over. I longed to give my boys a home that was ours, a place where they could feel safe and grounded, knowing it was just us. The reality of living in New York City came with a price tag I couldn't afford. Every time I looked at rental listings, my heart sank. The numbers were overwhelming, and I couldn't see how I could make it work, not on my own.

Kate had always been one of those friends who was always encouraging and would make light of a difficult situation. She lived in San Jose, California, and as a single parent herself, she understood the intricate dance of juggling work, kids, and the quest for personal fulfillment. Over one of our long phone calls, she floated an idea that lodged itself in the back of my mind: "If you ever want to move west, we could share a house. It might make things easier for both of us." At first, the thought seemed far-fetched. Uprooting my boys and leaving the familiarity of the East Coast for another city, another state in America, felt like a gamble. But the more I mulled it over, the more it seemed to align with what we needed: a fresh start, a chance to breathe again. I pictured life in California, its warm weather, a slower pace, and, most importantly, a support system in Kate. It felt scary but also deeply right. Staying in New York felt like clinging to a life that no longer fit.

Spring Break gave me the perfect window to explore this possibility. I decided to take the boys to San Jose and get a feel for what our lives there might look like. However, I wasn't prepared for the realities of traveling with kids. I didn't pack any snacks or sandwiches for the long flight, assuming they would feed us on the flight. Shortly after takeoff, the boys grew restless. Across the aisle, a woman and her daughter unwrapped sandwiches they must have picked up at the airport. Kwesi, my youngest, looked up at me as the flight attendant passed by with peanuts and said, "I don't want peanuts. Can I have my sandwich now?" My heart sank. I hadn't thought of bringing food, and there were no meals for sale on the flight. The flight attendant, noticing my distress, bent down and smiled at Kwesi. "I don't have sandwiches, sweetheart, but I can get you some cookies and chips. How does that sound?" Her kindness made all the difference. The boys settled down after their snack and eventually fell asleep, giving me a moment to breathe.

When we landed in San Jose, Kate and her children were there waiting for us with their warm smiles. The next day, I toured a couple of schools while the boys tagged along. They seemed excited about the prospect of the move, and I could feel my hesitation starting to fade away. San Jose had a charm that felt inviting, a place where I could envision us putting down roots. Our return ticket took us through San Francisco, and as we drove across the Golden Gate Bridge, the boys were captivated by the iconic red towers rising into the misty sky. This trip strengthened my determination. San Jose felt like a place I could move to with the boys.

The decision wasn't an easy one, though. Late at night, after the boys were asleep, I would sit by the window of our Brooklyn apartment we shared with Auntie Judy and Uncle Richie, staring out at the city lights and the constant hum of life outside. The familiar streets, the school just a short walk away, and the neighbors who had become part of our daily routine all tugged at my heart. I found myself wondering if I was doing the right thing. Moving across the country wasn't just about packing boxes and boarding a plane; it was about leaving behind the little stability we had fought so hard to build. I worried about the boys most of all. Kwesi and Kwame were young, but in their own way, they had begun to root themselves here. I couldn't help but feel the weight of guilt pressing down on me. Was I being selfish? Was I chasing something that might not even exist?

But deep down, I knew staying wasn't an option. Brooklyn felt like a safe place, but it also felt restricted. The cost of living loomed over every decision I made, and the city's relentless pace left me exhausted, yearning for space to breathe. More than anything, I wanted the boys to have a chance to thrive, to grow up in a place where they could see me at my best and hopefully build a life we could all be proud of. One night, after much deliberation, I picked up the phone and called Kate. "We're doing it," I said, my voice filled with relief. "I'm so proud of you," she said. "You're going to love it here, and we'll make this work together. You're not alone in this." Her encouragement was the balm I didn't realize I needed. For the first time in weeks, I allowed myself to imagine what life in San Jose might truly look like. Kate and I were both single mothers trying to make a way for our kids and ourselves, and now we would have each other. I began making plans and decluttering our belongings. The boys were too young to fully grasp what the move meant, but they sensed my growing excitement. Still, there were moments when the doubt crept back in, especially during quiet evenings when the reality of what we were leaving hit me hardest. I'd think about their little friends at school, the teachers who had been so patient and kind, and the routines we had built over the past few years. It felt like I was ripping them away from the small roots they had managed to plant. But then I would remind myself of why I was doing this: to give them a better future. As I packed our belongings, sorting through what to take and what to leave behind, I felt a mixture of sadness and hope. New York had served as a transitional phase, a location where I regained my balance after a challenging period, but it wasn't where our story would continue. San Jose was calling, and with it came the promise of a new beginning.

That night, as we gathered our belongings and made our way to the terminal at JFK, I felt a mixture of emotions swirling within me. The airport was buzzing with activity, the sounds of chatter and announcements filling the air, but all I could focus on were the tiny hands of my children clasped tightly in mine. As we approached the boarding gate, I glanced at their innocent faces, filled with excitement. We were stepping into the unknown again, but deep down, I knew God was always going before us. I usually recite Psalm 23 when I am anxious, so I began to recite it under my breath. This was our leap of faith, and I was ready to see where it would take us.

Chapter Eighteen

A NEW DAWN IN SAN JOSE

"Behold, I will do a new thing; now it shall spring forth;
shall ye not know it? I will even make a way in the
wilderness, and rivers in the desert."
— Isaiah 43:19 (KJV)

A s our plane landed in California, I felt a strong energy in the air. It hinted at the many possibilities this new place held for us. This move was not just a change of location; it marked the beginning of an emotional and spiritual journey. It was an adventure toward the life I had always wanted for myself and my children. Stepping off the plane, I felt the warm sun on my skin and a gentle breeze. The city welcomed us with its vibrant life and opportunities, and this was our chance to change our story. I imagined our new routines, my children laughing and playing in the warmth of our new community. We were ready to open our hearts and embrace this new chapter.

We looked forward to exploring our surroundings, meeting new people, and creating lasting memories. It was time for us to start over in a land full of possibilities and dreams just waiting to be fulfilled.

Settling in San Jose was filled with hope, resilience, and hard work for a brighter future for my boys and me. Our little house was humble but cozy, a shared space with Kate and her two children, who graciously welcomed us, and it quickly became a place where memories, laughter, and the sound of homework being done around the dining table filled the air. Finding the right school for my boys was the first big challenge, but I was determined to give them a stable and supportive environment. I decided to enroll my two boys in a small, community-oriented elementary school that my friend recommended. Her son also attended this school, which gave me some added confidence in my choice. The school was known for its nurturing environment and personalized attention, making it the perfect fit for my children's early education. I felt reassured knowing they would be in a place where they could flourish socially and academically.

The teachers were warm, attentive, and understood the importance of nurturing young minds with care and dedication. The boys' faces lit up when they saw the playground and met some friendly classmates, and I knew we were on the right path. I managed to secure a full-time position at San Jose Alternative School. This job aligned so well with my passion for education and my dedication to supporting students who needed an alternative approach. Yet, as fulfilling as this work was, it didn't quite meet all of our financial needs, so I took on a part-time job at Target. It was a juggle, but I made it work.

Every morning, I woke up before sunrise and spent time meditating and praying before I prepared for another long day. I'd pack lunches, lay out the boys' clothes, and make sure everyone was ready for the school day ahead. We'd pile into the car, the boys bubbling with energy, and head off on the morning commute. After dropping them off, I'd head to San Jose Alternative School, throwing myself into my work, teaching and mentoring students. I knew that every lesson, every bit of effort I put in, was not just helping my students but also laying the groundwork for my future career path. Still, the hours were long, and by the time I picked the boys up after school, I was already running on fumes. The afternoons were dedicated to homework, a ritual I took seriously, sitting at the kitchen table with the boys, helping them solve math problems or practice their spelling words. After dinner, my friend would step in to care for the boys while I headed off to my evening shift at Target. Those evenings were the hardest. As I boarded the bus, sadness and exhaustion would wash over me. The job at Target wasn't one I enjoyed; it was a necessity. California was expensive, and making ends meet required sacrifice. Weekends were no exception, and the weight of missing out on time with the boys or their activities often felt unbearable. I worried constantly that my absence in the evenings would create gaps in their lives, gaps I desperately wanted to fill with love, attention, and presence.

Sleep became a luxury I couldn't afford. I went to bed late and woke up early, my body operating on sheer determination. On weekends, I carved out time to take the boys and often my friend's son and his little sister to the library. It was one of the few places where we could be together, surrounded by books and possibilities. The boys loved it, and I loved our time together, which made my fatigue a little easier to bear. Living with my friend and her children was a blessing in disguise. Having our kids grow up together created a sense of community within our home. The boys adjusted well, and their bond with my friend's son brought stability I hadn't anticipated. Despite the challenges, those shared moments of laughter and play were very healthy for us.

Every day felt like a balancing act juggling work, parenting, and survival in a state where the cost of living weighed heavily on me. But through it all, I clung to the belief that this sacrifice was temporary. I prayed for the strength to keep going, to not miss out on the boys' lives, and to one day let go of the second job that kept me from them. My exhaustion was immense, but my resolve was greater. I was determined to make this life work, no matter how hard the road ahead seemed. One of the scriptures that gave me hope is Philippians 4:19 (KJV): "But my God shall supply all your needs according to his riches in glory by Christ Jesus."

That first Christmas in San Jose was a whirlwind of emotions. As the holiday approached, my boys and I were looking forward to the season, doing our best to embrace our new life, even with the memories of the past lingering. When my ex-husband mentioned he would be visiting, I prepared myself to navigate whatever complex feelings might come up, knowing that he hadn't seen the boys in a couple of years. But I was blindsided. He showed up, not alone as I had anticipated, but with the woman he'd left us for, someone who had once been part of our church family, someone I had welcomed into our home.

Seeing her there, with him, standing as a reminder of all we had endured, sent a flood of memories racing through me. My heart pounded, and I could barely keep my composure as the weight of those difficult years pressed down on me.

It wasn't just the betrayal itself; it was the sheer thoughtlessness of bringing her along, of presenting this new life so casually to our children after such a long absence. My mind swirled with emotions I thought I had settled, and I fought to keep the pain from showing, focusing instead on my boys. The confusion on their faces hurt me the most; they were just beginning to find a sense of security in our new life, and this visit stirred things that were too complex for them to fully understand. In that moment, I realized that no matter what, I would continue to protect their hearts and support them through every difficult transition. It was painful to revisit such deeply hurtful experiences, but it also reminded me of the strength I'd built over time and the resolve to continue moving forward, with or without the support of those from the past.

As he greeted us, offering a casual "hello" that felt impossibly out of place, I opened my mouth, but no words came out. Standing there, frozen in that moment, all the words, all the anger, and the pain I wanted to express felt lodged in my throat. I glanced at my boys, who stood expectantly beside me, their innocent faces unaware of the emotional weight crushing me. So instead of speaking, I gently nudged them forward toward their father, plastering on a weak smile. I told him I'd pick them up after church and, with a last look at my boys, turned and walked away.

Driving off, the dam of emotions I'd held back burst, and I wept. Tears streamed down my face, blurring the Christmas lights and decorations as I drove, each one a cruel reminder of the shattered family and life we'd once shared. The anguish was overwhelming; memories of betrayal, disappointment, and the painful realization of the brokenness he had brought into our lives played on repeat in my mind. Arriving at the church for the Christmas Eve service, I hoped the familiar sanctuary might bring some solace. Yet, as the music filled the room, each hymn seemed to amplify my heartache. I prayed with all my might, pleading for strength, for healing, and for the grace to release the bitterness weighing so heavily on my soul. After the service, I felt a fragile calm settle over me, a small piece of comfort as I headed to pick up the boys. They were waiting in the hotel lobby, their little faces lighting up as they saw me, though I could tell they had questions. As we buckled into the car, my youngest turned to me, his innocent voice piercing the silence.

"Mom, who is that lady with Dad?" The question hung in the air, and I felt my heart twist. Not wanting to burden him with the truth, I forced a smile and replied, "Oh, she's just a business partner."

Even as I spoke, a wave of shame washed over me. I'd always promised myself I'd be honest with my boys, that I'd shelter them from as much pain as possible but still teach them to face life's challenges head-on. Yet here I was, unable to reveal the reality of the situation. Christmas morning arrived, and I woke with a heaviness pressing down on my chest, a mix of sorrow and strength colliding within me. The plan was for their father to take the boys for the day, but as the morning came, I couldn't bear the thought of them spending Christmas with him and her. So, I called, asking that he pick them up in the evening instead and take them to a movie after our Christmas dinner. It was all I could manage to keep this part of the holiday for us, without the shadows of old memories intruding. When the boys woke up, their laughter and excitement filled the house as they eagerly tore into their gifts. We enjoyed a hearty breakfast, as was our tradition, and settled down to watch *The Sound of Music*. It was the same movie we watched every Christmas, a comforting piece of familiarity in our changing lives, the music and story carrying us away for a while, reminding us of Germany somehow.

That evening, I took the boys to meet their father. I kissed them both and watched them walk away, feeling the ache of letting them go even for a few hours. While they were at the movies, I lingered in the quiet, reflecting on the strength I needed to hold onto for myself and them. My ex-husband left soon afterward, taking his new wife with him and heading back to the life he'd chosen. And though there was relief in seeing him go, I knew I was left with something greater to carry. In that quiet moment, I decided I couldn't let bitterness or resentment poison this new life we were building in San Jose. I needed to let go of the hurt, piece by piece, and find a way to forgive. Not for him, but for me, and for the life I was determined to give my boys. Forgiveness wouldn't be easy, but I resolved to work at it, to turn the page, to create a life in San Jose that was grounded in love, resilience, and new beginnings.

As the holiday season ended, we slipped back into the familiar rhythm of our daily lives. I returned to my role at the San Jose Alternative School, while the boys immersed themselves in their studies. I made the difficult decision to leave my position at Target; the relentless pace of retail during the holidays had taken its toll on me. The emotional undercurrents of the season, with its mixture of joy and nostalgia, left me drained. Choosing to step away felt liberating, a chance to reclaim precious moments to spend with my boys, even if it meant navigating the tightrope of a tighter budget. Living in California, however, increasingly weighed on me as the months rolled by. Life's everyday costs just kept going up, seeming to hang over us like a big, dark cloud. Despite holding down a full-time job, the reality of our finances often felt like a weight pressing down, making it seem as if we were merely treading water. I was determined to create a meaningful life for us here, but our financial situation was a major concern that overshadowed our goals.

Spring Break brought a much-needed change of scenery for me and the boys. We traveled to sunny Florida, where we spent a week reconnecting with my close friend Helen. The moment we arrived, the warm, salty breeze and the sound of waves crashing against the shore wrapped around us like a comforting embrace. Being with Helen was like a breath of fresh air; we dove into long, heartfelt conversations over fresh seafood dinners and afternoons spent lounging by the pool. We laughed until our sides hurt, reminiscing about old times as if no years had passed us by. Our discussions often turned to the pressing issue of the cost of living. Helen painted a picture of Florida that felt inviting, a landscape where life seemed a bit more manageable. I could envision us thriving in a place with vibrant communities and a lower cost of living, where the dream of establishing a secure and sustainable future didn't feel so distant.

As we strolled on the clear-water beach, I found myself daydreaming about the possibilities of affordable housing, a slower pace of life, and the chance to build something lasting. Returning to the familiar yet hectic environment of California after that trip was jarring. My mind was filled with thoughts about my life in San Jose, but Florida seemed like an exciting option, tempting me to think about a new chapter with more possibilities. For now, I would focus on the present and enjoy my time with the boys and our friends. However, Helen's wise words and the idea of a more affordable and fulfilling life in Florida took root in my mind, planting a seed of possibility that promised to grow in the coming days.

After returning to California, I shared my idea of moving with Kate during one of our long conversations, I could see a spark of excitement in her eyes. She, too, was feeling the pull southward, yearning for a fresh start away from the hustle and bustle of our current lives. With her encouragement and shared enthusiasm, I finally made the decision to relocate to Florida once the school year ended. Keeping the boys settled in school for the remainder of the year felt right, allowing them to finish out their classes without interruption and providing them with a sense of stability as we prepared for this significant change. It was important to me that they had a smooth transition, especially considering how much they loved their current school and friends.

I asked Helen if she could help me find an apartment in Florida, and we quickly dove into the planning process. With her extensive knowledge of the area, she began scouting various neighborhoods, sending me a steady stream of photos and listings. Meanwhile, I focused on the nitty-gritty details that come with such a big move, researching school transfer requirements for my kids and meticulously budgeting for the expenses ahead, including moving costs and potential living expenses. With each listing Helen shared, the decision felt more tangible and increasingly like the right path forward. It was a bittersweet realization that we would soon be leaving San Jose, a vibrant city where we had poured our energy and passion into rebuilding our lives once again after the challenges we faced. Yet, amid the nostalgia, the excitement of a new beginning in Florida, where the sun shone brighter, friendships awaited, and the cost of living was significantly more affordable, filled me with renewed hope and positive energy.

Chapter Nineteen

A NEW BEGINNING
IN FLORIDA

"The Lord Himself goes before you and will be with you;
He will never leave you nor forsake you.
Do not be afraid; do not be discouraged."
—Deuteronomy 31:8 (NIV)

The move from San Jose to Florida culminated in months of planning, packing, and countless goodbyes to the new friends the boys had made. The decision to leave California hadn't been easy, especially after working hard to build a stable life for my boys in San Jose. Yet, between the cost of living and my longing for a more balanced environment for them, it was time to start fresh once again. The semester was coming to a close, and the boys were wrapping up another chapter in their young lives. Kwame had completed fourth grade, and Kwesi was graduating from kindergarten, a milestone marked by a special graduation ceremony. I arrived at the school auditorium early, slipping quietly into a seat at the back with Kwame, hoping to remain unnoticed.

The ceremony was a joyful occasion, filled with proud parents, laughter, and the innocent excitement of children. As the program progressed, a slideshow of family photos began playing on the big screen. Each picture celebrated the unique stories of the families present. When our turn came, the screen displayed a photo of just the three of us: me, Kwame, and Kwesi. A lump formed in my throat. I was sure no one else gave our photo a second thought, but to me, it was a reminder of our incomplete family. Shame washed over me. I felt as though I had failed my boys, that I couldn't give them the intact family they deserved. My tears flowed freely, though I tried to wipe them away discreetly. I wept not just for myself but for Kwame and Kwesi, who were growing up without their dad's daily presence. It was a grief I carried silently, tucked away beneath the surface of my busy life. Yet, amidst the swirl of negative emotions, there was a glimmer of pride. Kwesi's name was called, and he walked across the stage to receive his diploma, his little face alight with pride and accomplishment. He had done it! He graduated from kindergarten and was ready for first grade. I clapped with all the enthusiasm I could muster, my heart swelling with love and pride for my son. The ceremony ended, and Kwesi ran to me and Kwame, his face glowing with joy. Kwame hugged him tightly, and Kwesi proudly showed off his diploma.

When I booked our flight, I had been so wrapped up in the details of moving that I completely overlooked the time difference. Our tickets had a layover in South Carolina, not a direct flight as I'd hoped. We arrived at the airport late at night, with just enough time to get through security and make it to our gate. I was already feeling exhausted, but my boys were troupers as we boarded the plane in California and settled in for the first leg of our journey. When we landed in South Carolina around 1:30 a.m., it felt as though the world had been stripped of color and sound, with the fluorescent airport lights casting a cold, empty glow across the nearly deserted terminal. I realized we had a four-hour layover, and a tired wave of frustration washed over me. I looked down at the boys, hoping they might stay awake for the long walk to our next gate, but they were both fast asleep.

With my youngest boy soundly slumbering, his small body heavy in my arms, I attempted to gently rouse my older son, hoping he could manage the trek. He opened his eyes, his face crinkling in that hazy confusion between sleep and wakefulness as he stumbled beside me holding my hand. I tried to coax him along, but he was mostly sleepwalking, his feet barely moving as he leaned on me, exhausted beyond words. It felt as if we were the only souls in that endless stretch of airport corridors, each step an effort against the rising ache in my arms and back. Every minute stretched into an eternity, and I felt the weight of everything – not just the boys, but the weight of leaving San Jose, the uncertainties of the move, the reality of having to do this alone. I kept walking, determined to make it through the long hallways, past the stores closed for the night, the rows of empty chairs, and the eerie silence punctuated only by the faint hum of airport machinery. At some point, I felt a few tears slip down my cheeks, catching me off guard. I didn't mean to cry.

But here, in this deserted airport with two sleepy boys depending on me, the tears came quietly, a mixture of exhaustion, sadness, and the overwhelming responsibility I carried.

We finally reached our gate and sank into the cold, hard seats. I sat between the boys, one leaning heavily on each side, their warmth a small comfort in that lonely place. As they dozed, I let myself breathe, looking around the empty terminal and giving in to the loneliness I felt. It was a rare moment where the enormity of our journey caught up with me, but I reminded myself why we were doing this. For a better life, for the chance to rebuild yet again in a place where I hoped we could finally put down roots. By the time the announcement for boarding our flight to Tampa crackled over the intercom, I had gathered myself. The boys stirred as I gently woke them up, my arms numb from holding them close. We finally boarded, and as I watched the sun begin to rise over the wing of the plane, I knew that no matter the difficulties, we were going to be all right. We were on our way to a new chapter, and we were together.

When we touched down at Tampa International Airport, I felt a surge of both relief and anticipation. The weight of the journey finally lifted as we collected our luggage and made our way to the arrivals area. The boys, though groggy from the flight, perked up when they spotted Helen waiting for us, her familiar, warm smile a comforting sight. She waved excitedly, and the boys ran to greet her, laughing as she bent to hug them. I felt a rush of gratitude. She had been such a solid presence in my life, and here she was again, ready to help us settle into our new chapter.

As we loaded our bags into her car and buckled the boys into their seats, Helen suggested a short detour before heading to Haines City. "I thought you might like a little view of the water," she said with a smile. I was instantly intrigued. A glimpse of the coast felt like the perfect way to begin this new journey in Florida, so I nodded eagerly, and we set off toward St. Petersburg. The boys' faces lit up as we approached the Howard Frankland Bridge, which stretched elegantly over the water. The bright morning sun glistened on the waves, and the gentle rise and fall of the road seemed to mirror our excitement. The boys pressed their faces against the windows, wide-eyed as they took in the endless expanse of blue on either side. They giggled and pointed, chattering excitedly about the boats they could see dotting the water and the birds swooping above us. I couldn't help but smile, watching them soak in this new experience.

As we drove back from the coast, Helen suggested stopping for breakfast, and I quickly agreed. We pulled up to a cozy, family-owned restaurant that looked like it had been there for generations. We took our seats, and the boys eagerly scanned the menu. I could see the excitement still glowing in their eyes from the drive. They each chose pancakes, and soon enough, their plates arrived, piled high with fluffy stacks, drizzled in syrup, and topped with whipped cream and strawberries. Helen and I sipped coffee and caught up while the boys enjoyed their breakfast. I told her about our journey and the big changes ahead. I felt a sense of hope, sitting there with my friend and my children. After breakfast, we packed up and hit the road once more, now bound for Haines City. Helen drove, showing us the areas as we passed through neighborhoods, parks, and orange groves. The boys listened intently, their excitement shifting from the bridge and the water to the idea of our new home.

We finally arrived at Helen's home. Stepping out of the car and taking in the bright Florida sunshine, I felt ready. Ready for what, I didn't fully know, but the weight of the journey, the endless miles, the moments of doubt, and the tears shed quietly during the layover in South Carolina were all part of my story. The air was warm, tinged with heavy humidity. I tightly held Kwame's and Kwesi's hands, my two anchors through it all. My heart whispered my favorite scripture: "For I know the plans I have for you, declares the Lord, plans to prosper you and not to harm you, plans to give you hope and a future" (Jeremiah 29:11). Helen and her family welcomed us with open arms.

My days in Florida were filled with to-do lists, my mind a symphony of logistics: finding schools, securing a job, and carving out a sense of normalcy for the boys. Education was my top priority. Kwame was about to enter fifth grade, and Kwesi, still so small and curious, was heading into first. Their future depended on solid schooling, and I was determined to give them the best I could manage. I discovered the concept of magnet schools and was intrigued. The promise of specialized programs and smaller class sizes seemed like a perfect fit for my boys. I applied with high hopes, but the admissions process was a lottery, a game of chance. My heart sank when the results came back, and neither Kwame nor Kwesi had been selected. Disappointed but undeterred, I turned my attention to charter schools. After visiting a few, I chose a small one that felt warm and welcoming. The boys adjusted quickly.

As the boys settled into their new routines, I threw myself into finding us a home. Living with Helen was a blessing, but I craved a space solely ours, a haven where we could shut the door and breathe deeply without the lingering awareness of being guests. After weeks of searching, we found it: a modest two-bedroom apartment with white walls that seemed to glow with potential. It wasn't much, but it was ours. The boys shared a bedroom, filling it quickly with their books, toys, and laughter. I often heard them giggling late into the night, a sound that filled my heart with joy and relief. I claimed the smaller bedroom as my retreat, decorating it simply with a bed and a desk where I could study and plan. For the first time since leaving Heidelberg, we had a place we could call home, no borrowed corners or shared living spaces, just the three of us under one roof. It was humbling but also empowering. I cooked meals in our tiny kitchen, the aroma of jollof rice or fried plantains wafting through the air. With the boys' education squared away and a roof over our heads, the next step was to find work. Teaching had always been my calling, but the demands of being a full-time single parent required flexibility. Substituting was the perfect fit. It allowed me to earn a steady income while being present for Kwame and Kwesi when they needed me most.

Every morning, I woke up early to pack their lunches and drop them off at school before heading to whatever classroom needed me that day. No two days were the same. Sometimes I was teaching at an elementary school and other days, I was teaching reading at a middle school. It was challenging but also invigorating. Teaching reminded me of my purpose and gave me the confidence to keep moving forward. Still, I knew that this was only the beginning. My dreams extended far beyond substitute teaching. I had paused my education during the turbulence of the past few years, but now it was time to pick up where I left off. I enrolled at the local community college, determined to finish my degree. My nights were spent at the kitchen table, textbooks spread out in front of me while the boys slept. Life in Florida was far from easy, but it was ours to shape. We still visited Helen's family often; their home was where we met to cook meals and gather for the kids to play.

Chapter Twenty

ROOTED IN FAITH, GROWING IN GRACE

"They will be called oaks of righteousness, a planting of the Lord for the display of His splendor."
— Isaiah 61:3 (NIV)

Winter Haven began to feel like home in ways I hadn't imagined. Among the milestones in our new life, finding a church was one of the most significant. After weeks of searching, we discovered a welcoming congregation in Lakeland. From the moment we stepped into the sanctuary, I felt a connection, a stirring in my spirit that told me this was where we were meant to be. The music was uplifting, the sermons filled with wisdom, and the sense of community was genuine. Sundays became a time of renewal and grounding. I would drop Kwame and Kwesi off at the children's church, where they joined other children in singing, crafts, and learning

Bible stories. They loved it, their smiles and stories on the drive home proof they were forming friendships and growing in their faith. While the boys were occupied, I attended the adult service. The pastor's words often felt as though they were directed at me, speaking to the struggles and triumphs of my journey. I would cry throughout the sermon. It was a space where I could reflect, exhale, and recharge for the week ahead.

One Sunday, the announcement about volunteering caught my attention. I had always believed in the power of giving back, and this seemed like the perfect way to deepen my connection with the church while nurturing my spiritual life. I signed up to volunteer with the children's ministry, deciding to teach children's church for a while. Teaching was familiar territory for me and combining it with faith felt natural. I loved creating lessons that brought Bible stories to life, using songs, skits, and crafts to engage the little ones. Their enthusiasm was contagious, and I often found myself learning from their unfiltered faith and joy. Volunteering gave me a sense of purpose beyond my day-to-day responsibilities. It was healing to be part of a group that valued faith, kindness, and community. My heart felt lighter with every Sunday spent in fellowship and service. During one of the services, the pastor spoke about the importance of deepening one's knowledge of the Word. He mentioned a Bible study course the church was offering, designed to help members build a stronger foundation in their faith. Intrigued, I signed up. The course met once a week in the evenings, and it quickly became a highlight of my routine. I would have the boys do their homework in the church. Each session was a deep dive into Scripture, exploring its historical context, its lessons for daily life, and its application to our spiritual growth. The discussions were rich and thought-provoking, and I found myself connecting spiritually.

Studying the Bible in this structured way strengthened my faith and provided me with tools to navigate the challenges of single motherhood. Verses that I had read countless times took on new meaning, offering wisdom and reassurance that God's plan for my life was unfolding, even if I couldn't yet see the full picture.

The church became more than a place of worship; it became a cornerstone of our lives. I formed friendships with other parents and volunteers who understood the complexities of raising children while balancing work, school, and personal growth. We supported each other through prayer, shared meals, and long conversations after Bible study. The boys often grew frustrated with me because I enjoyed chatting with friends after church services. While I relished those moments of connection and fellowship, they were always eager to leave, their stomachs grumbling with hunger. As soon as the last song echoed through the sanctuary, they tugged impatiently at my sleeve, wanting to rush past the lobby rather than pause for conversation. To them, talking to friends after church service was secondary to the urgent call for lunch.

Kwame and Kwesi thrived in the church community. They participated in children's events, like Vacation Bible School and holiday programs, where they made friends. Volunteering, studying, and building relationships at church anchored me during those early years in Florida. I began to see the small, steady ways God was working in our lives: the kind smiles of church members who became friends, the peace I felt during prayer, and the strength I gained from serving others. For so long, my journey had been one of survival, constantly moving forward without much time to process the pain or celebrate the victories. Now, in Winter Haven, I found moments of stillness and gratitude. This was more than just a new chapter in a new state; it was a rebirth of faith, community, and hope. Slowly but surely, we were building a life rooted in resilience and grace.

The months flew by, and the boys were accepted to All Saints Academy. Kwesi began third grade, and Kwame sixth grade. I realized that private school was a bit different in the United States. I attended a private boarding school in Ghana, but the culture here in the United States was different. We revered our teachers, and respecting our elders was very important to my culture. It was very important to teach the boys to speak their minds when an adult negatively questioned them but also to know how to respond without being disrespectful. Our first semester at All Saints Academy was great. The boys made friends and adjusted very well to the school's culture. After the Christmas holidays, Kwesi's teacher asked the students what they did for the Christmas break, but then she asked Kwesi to share how he celebrated Kwanzaa.

The question took Kwesi by surprise because, at the time, he knew nothing about Kwanzaa. Even though I am from Ghana, it does not mean I celebrate Kwanzaa. So, I researched Kwanzaa and found out that it was a very cool holiday created in 1966 by Dr. Maulana Karenga, an African American activist, and scholar, to celebrate African American history and culture and to promote unity and empowerment in the African American community.

How cool is that! I decided to have a meeting with the teacher to enlighten her on the celebration of Kwanzaa and make her aware that Ghanaians also celebrate Christmas. I explained that although Kwanzaa is an important and meaningful holiday, it is not widely celebrated in African countries, including Ghana. The teacher listened attentively, and our conversation sparked a much larger dialogue about the importance of understanding and celebrating diversity in the classroom.

The meeting sparked an engaging and fruitful dialogue with another parent whose children also attended All Saints Academy. She expressed her concerns about the prevalent cultural assumptions and the urgency of broadening our students' worldviews. Energized by our shared vision, we decided to take proactive steps and approached the head of the lower school with a compelling proposal: to host an International Day. To our delight, the school embraced the idea with enthusiasm and support. Each class eagerly adopted a different country, and students dove into researching its unique culture, rich traditions, and exciting festivities. They crafted eye-catching posters and vibrant visual displays to highlight the history, iconic landmarks, delectable foods, and diverse languages of their selected nations. On the day of the event, the school gymnasium was transformed into a dazzling cultural fair, filled with colorful decorations, lively presentations, and the enticing aromas of international cuisine. The atmosphere buzzed with excitement as students proudly showcased their hard work and shared their newfound knowledge, creating an unforgettable experience for the whole community.

Tables were adorned with flags, traditional artifacts, and delicious foods from all over the world. Students dressed in traditional attire presented their projects and shared interesting facts they had learned about their adopted countries. The atmosphere was electric with curiosity, pride, and joy. Parents, teachers, and students moved from table to table, tasting new foods, listening to cultural music, and asking questions. Kwesi's class represented three countries: Nigeria, Ghana, and Liberia. As I walked through the event, I couldn't help but smile. This was more than just a school project; it was a celebration of diversity and an opportunity for children to learn that the world is so much bigger than their own experiences. I saw pride on the faces of students as they shared what they had learned. Parents, too, were excited to see their children embrace new cultures and perspectives. Later that evening, as we drove home, Kwesi and I reminisced about how wonderful it was to celebrate the different countries represented.

I had been fortunate to experience different cultures, and I wanted the same for my boys. I knew that understanding and appreciating diversity would enrich their lives and open doors to new opportunities. International Day became an annual tradition at All Saints Academy. Each year, it grew bigger and better, with more families participating and more countries represented. It became a day where students celebrated not only their heritage but also the beautiful, diverse tapestry of cultures that make up our world. Looking back, that simple question from Kwesi's teacher about Kwanzaa sparked something extraordinary. One lesson I took from this was the importance of speaking up, educating others, and creating opportunities for cultural exchange. By sharing our stories and learning from one another, we can build bridges of understanding and appreciation that transcend borders and backgrounds. For the boys and me, International Day was not just a school event, it was a reflection of our lives, our journeys, and the rich, multicultural world we are proud to be a part of.

Chapter Twenty-One

A SEASON OF GROWTH AND TRANSFORMATION

"Being confident of this, that He who began a
good work in you will carry it on to completion
until the day of Christ Jesus."
— Philippians 1:6 (NIV)

The Newton boys' summers in Winter Haven were jam-packed with excitement and growth. Each day was filled with enriching activities, from perfecting their strokes in swimming lessons at the community pool to diving into adventurous tales during the summer reading program at the library. They eagerly volunteered to organize bookshelves and host story time sessions for younger children and spent afternoons preparing meals and distributing them to the homeless. These experiences not only kept them busy but also fostered a strong sense of responsibility and compassion. I enrolled them in swimming, summer reading, volunteering at the library, and feeding the homeless. Teaching the boys about altruism was very important to me because I wanted them to understand the value of giving back and how small acts of kindness can have a profound impact on others. I believed that learning to serve others would shape their character, instilling empathy and a sense of responsibility. Altruism became a guiding principle in their lives, shaping them into compassionate and thoughtful individuals.

While living in NYC, we would go to serve Christmas meals to single mothers and their children living in the shelter. The City Hall Restaurant organized the event, and my sister-in-law would take us there to volunteer. The ambiance was wonderful, with the mayor and dignitaries stopping by to speak with the mothers and the volunteers. The mayor paused to thank the volunteers, sharing how impactful these efforts were in the lives of the shelter residents. The boys and I took a photo with the mayor, and meeting all these people made each visit feel truly special. After settling in Florida, we would visit NYC during the Christmas holidays and still go to the City Hall on Christmas Eve to serve meals. These trips became an anchor for our family traditions, reinforcing the values of service and community. For the boys, it was a great time to visit NYC to see all the Christmas decorations and the Rockettes at Radio City Music Hall. As they grew older, they took on more responsibilities during the events, such as greeting guests or helping organize supplies.

On New Year's Eve, after the midnight service, we went to have breakfast at Perkins, a restaurant that was always bustling with late-night customers. As we waited to be served, I decided to write down a ten-year goal and share it with the boys. I told them my plan: I would work toward earning my bachelor's, master's, and doctorate. Within five years of moving to our apartment, I would buy a house, a place we could truly call home. Most importantly, I vowed to help the boys excel in their studies so they could be accepted into college with full scholarships. They looked at me proudly and started telling me about their goals. Their excitement seemed a bit over the top. With this vision in mind, I poured myself into my studies and eventually achieved my dream of becoming a teacher. I graduated with my first degree.

The college interviewed me for a story to be published, and because the college became a four-year institution, the local news used my story to encourage other single mothers. I used every resource the college offered, from tutoring to study groups and studying with my boys at the local library on Saturday mornings. A photographer from the college asked to take photos of me and the boys for the newspapers. My story was celebrated as a single mom who accomplished her goal while raising two boys far from her home country. On my graduation day, Auntie Judy flew in with her husband, Uncle Richie, to celebrate this milestone. My friends also attended the ceremony. Their presence filled me with gratitude and joy; it reminded me of the supportive community I had built. My boys were very proud to see me walk across the stage to receive my diploma.

My first full-time teaching job was with a kindergarten class. My friend Connie helped me decorate my classroom with a butterfly theme. Walking into the bright, colorful classroom on the first day, I was filled with excitement. The walls were adorned with cheerful posters, and tiny chairs were neatly arranged around low tables. I could hear the faint giggles of children as they arrived with their backpacks, some clutching their parents' hands tightly. But as the day unfolded, I was completely unprepared for the reality of teaching five-year-olds. I was shocked when many of them couldn't even write their names. I remember standing there, feeling utterly overwhelmed, wondering what I had gotten myself into. That evening, I called Connie and vented my frustration. Laughing, she said, "Vivian, you are not teaching high school kids!" We both burst into laughter at how absurd my complaints sounded. Her words put things into perspective, and I realized I needed to adjust my expectations. With the guidance of two amazing kindergarten teachers, I slowly found my rhythm. They showed me how to break tasks into simple, engaging steps and how to celebrate small victories with the kids. The joy on their faces when they mastered something new became my greatest reward. Each morning, as I greeted my little students, their energy and curiosity were all I needed to get through the day. Meanwhile, the boys were also making great strides. Kwame, with his quiet determination, was preparing to step into high school, while Kwesi, ever the curious and lively one, was moving on to middle school.

The semester came to an end with my little kindergarteners doing very well with their assessments, and they were ready for first grade. I ended my first teaching year with gratitude but decided to move on to teaching middle school. It felt like the right decision to explore a new challenge and expand my teaching experience. It was also the last day for the boys at their school, and Kwame was stepping into ninth grade. He was set to receive a few awards at the closing ceremony, so I made it a point to attend. A couple of friends came along to support me, knowing how much this moment meant. When Kwame's name was called several times for different awards, I couldn't help but beam with pride. Each time he walked up to the stage, I clapped harder, feeling an indescribable sense of accomplishment and joy. At that moment, I felt a sense of pride I had not experienced since my divorce. For years, I had carried the heaviness of being a single mom, a weight that seemed to press down on me at every school function. I often felt a tinge of shame not because I had done anything wrong, but because of the societal expectations and judgments that seemed to surround single motherhood. It felt as though every glance and question carried an unspoken commentary about my life and choices. But this day was different.

As I watched Kwame stand tall, confident, and deserving of his accolades, that heaviness lifted. Instead of shame, I felt pride pure, unfiltered pride. My boys were thriving. They were not going to be a statistic. They were living proof of resilience, determination, and the power of love and hard work. As we drove home that evening, the awards safely tucked in the back seat, I glanced at Kwame through the rearview mirror. He was chatting excitedly with his brother, the two of them making plans for the summer. My heart swelled with gratitude. For the first time in a long while, I allowed myself to celebrate their success and my own. While the boys were out for the summer, Kwame attended a summer program at the University of South Florida for STEM, and Kwesi attended a robotics camp. I had begun researching programs with scholarships earlier in the year so the boys could be engaged during the summer. There were so many programs for students, but each required an application, an essay, and submission of grades to be evaluated and chosen. It was a daunting process, but I was determined to give the boys productive and fun summers. I wanted them to dream big and realize that opportunities were within their reach if they were willing to work for them. Kwame thrived in the STEM program, coming home excited about projects and experiments. Kwesi, meanwhile, found a passion for robotics and proudly showed me the robots he had designed in the program.

This season was for growth and transformation for me and the boys. For me, graduating from college was not just the achievement of earning a degree but a symbol of reclaiming my life after years of challenges. For the boys, it was a summer of exploration, self-discovery, and inspiration for their futures. But the journey to that summer was not without its obstacles. Financial difficulties loomed large throughout my academic and career pursuits. As a single mom, every dollar was carefully budgeted. There were days when it was difficult to make ends meet. I often took on part-time jobs in addition to my coursework and parenting responsibilities. The stress of juggling these roles was overwhelming at times, but I remained steadfast that I was building a better future for my family.

Time management was another constant struggle. My days were a whirlwind of dropping the boys off at school, attending my classes, working, and helping the boys with homework in the evenings. Late at night, when the house was quiet, I would sit at the kitchen table, poring over textbooks and writing essays, often fueled by little more than coffee and determination. There were moments when exhaustion threatened to consume me, but I pressed on, knowing that my perseverance was setting an example for my boys. Professional setbacks also tested my resolve. As I sought different jobs and part-time jobs in my field, I faced rejections that were difficult to bear. Employers sometimes overlooked my potential because of the gaps in my resume caused by my years as a stay-at-home mom. Others questioned my ability to balance work and parenting. These experiences were disheartening, but they also fueled my determination to prove my worth and succeed against the odds. Through it all, my boys were my greatest motivation. Their smiles, hugs, and belief in me reminded me why I embarked on this journey. Every obstacle I faced became a steppingstone toward achieving my dreams and providing the Newton boys with a life filled with opportunities and love.

My graduation was not the end of my story but the beginning of a new chapter. I had plans to pursue further education, to obtain a master's degree in a field that allowed me to make a meaningful impact in my community and eventually my doctorate. I also explored ways to support other single mothers, sharing my experiences to inspire and empower them to pursue their dreams despite the odds. For Kwame and Kwesi, I continued to seek out opportunities that would nurture their talents and passions.

Chapter Twenty-Two

THE HOUSE THAT
FAITH BUILT

"Unless the Lord builds the house, the builders labor in vain."
— Psalm 127:1 (NIV)

One of my greatest aspirations was about to be realized. For years, I had dreamed of owning a home, a place where my boys and I could create lasting memories, a sanctuary that would be ours. When we moved into our apartment, I promised the boys that within five years, we would have our own home. It was a promise rooted in determination, faith, and countless hours of preparation. I had spent years working diligently to improve my credit and educate myself on the nuances of being a first-time homebuyer. I attended workshops, read books, and consulted friends who had walked this path before me. I learned about saving for a down payment, understanding mortgage terms, and the importance of finding the right location. By the time we were ready to begin our search, I felt equipped and confident.

One sunny Saturday morning, we set out to find our future home. A dear friend introduced me to a real estate agent, a kind and knowledgeable woman who immediately understood what I was looking for. It was important to me that our new home had a backyard where the boys could play, a space to host friends, and perhaps even a little garden. Just as crucial was proximity to the boys' school to ensure our mornings remained as seamless as possible. The agent picked us up early that morning, and we spent the day driving through neighborhoods, stopping at various houses that fit within our budget. The first few houses were nice but didn't feel quite right. Either the yards were too small, or the commute to school would be too long. I wanted a house that felt like home the moment we stepped inside.

By mid-afternoon, we pulled into a new development not far from the boys' school. The moment we arrived, I knew this could be it. The area was quiet and safe, with tree-lined streets and a sense of community. The real estate agent explained that the homes here were being built from the ground up, which meant we would have the chance to choose the lot and customize certain features. My excitement soared as we toured the model homes, imagining where we would place our furniture and how the boys would decorate their rooms. The following week, we returned to the development to select our lot. The boys were buzzing with excitement, running around, and debating which spot they liked best. After careful consideration, I chose a lot with a spacious backyard. Standing there, I could already envision summer evenings with the boys playing outside while I watched from the patio. It felt like a dream inching closer to reality.

Construction began a few weeks later. I made it a point to stop by the site regularly, chatting with the builders and watching the progress. The boys often joined me after school, eagerly pointing out where their rooms would be and imagining all the adventures they'd have. Those visits became a ritual, a way to stay connected to the journey and celebrate each small milestone. The smell of fresh wood and the hum of construction equipment filled me with anticipation. Months later, the day arrived for us to walk through the nearly finished house. My friend Helen accompanied us as we inspected every detail, from the layout of the kitchen to the fixtures in the bathrooms. We chose the appliances together, and the boys had a say in the color of their bedroom walls. Their excitement was contagious as they talked about how they would arrange their furniture and which posters they would hang.

The house was completed a few weeks later, and I scheduled the closing appointment to sign the papers. On the big day, I took the boys with me. We dressed up for the occasion, knowing it was a moment we'd remember forever. Sitting in the office, pen in hand, I felt a wave of emotions: gratitude, pride, and an overwhelming sense of accomplishment. When the final signature was in place, the agent handed us the keys. The boys cheered, and I couldn't help but shed a few tears of joy.

The moving day was a flurry of activity and excitement. My dear friend Helen and her family came over to help us pack. Together, we boxed up years of memories from our apartment, laughing and reminiscing as we worked. By the time we arrived at the new house, the sun was beginning to set, casting a warm glow over our new home. Unpacking was a team effort. The boys eagerly carried their belongings to their rooms, claiming their spaces and arranging their things just so. That evening, we sat on the living room floor surrounded by boxes, eating pizza and talking about all the possibilities that lay ahead. As the boys settled into their beds that night, I lay on my air mattress, overwhelmed by a profound sense of fulfillment. Tears streamed down my face, and I couldn't hold them back. This home was more than just a structure; it was a testament to our journey, a symbol of perseverance and faith. We had achieved a milestone that once seemed so far out of reach, and it was only the beginning of the memories we would create within these walls. My prayer that night was a simple "Thank you, God."

My Step-by-Step Plan for Buying My First Home
Set a Clear Goal

- Define Your Vision: Identify what you want in a home. Consider location, size, type, and amenities like a backyard or proximity to schools.
- Establish a Timeline: Set a realistic timeline for achieving your goal. For instance, I aimed to buy my home within five years.
- Build Credit: Work on improving your credit score. Pay off debts, avoid late payments, and maintain a healthy credit utilization ratio.
- Save for a Down Payment: Create a separate savings account for your down payment and closing costs. Automate contributions to stay consistent.

- Research Assistance Programs: Explore first-time homebuyer programs in your area that may offer grants or lower down payment requirements.
- Create a Budget: Factor in all costs, including mortgage payments, property taxes, homeowners' insurance, and maintenance.
- Take Homebuyer Education Courses: Many organizations offer workshops or online courses for first-time buyers.
- Choose a Lender: Research lenders and compare rates. Look for one that offers good terms for first-time buyers.
- Review Documents: Carefully read all paperwork, including the mortgage agreement and deed.
- Celebrate the Moment: Pick up your keys and step into your new home with joy and gratitude.

Chapter Twenty-Three

BUILDING A VILLAGE OF FRIENDSHIPS AND SISTERHOOD

"Two are better than one because they have a good
return for their labor: If either of them falls down,
one can help the other up."
— Ecclesiastes 4:9-10 (NIV)

A s a single parent living far away from family and friends, it was very important for me to build a support group of friends who could step in to help me when I needed that help. Living in a foreign land that I now called home, it was important that I immerse myself in the community. I made friends with the mothers from the boys' school and some from church. These remarkable women became very involved with me and the boys. There were times when the boys were involved in separate after-school programs, and I could not attend both. I would contact a parent whose child was also in the program to take pictures and support my kid. The parents at All Saints Academy were very kind and jumped in to assist without hesitation. My weekends were hectic; Kwame might have a chess competition, and Kwesi might have a robotics competition. I would drop off Kwame, and the other parents would bring him home after the competition while I stayed to support Kwesi.

Building a village of friendship did not happen overnight. It required consistent effort, trust, and reciprocity. I began by engaging with the parents during school events. I introduced myself, shared stories about my boys, and showed genuine interest in their lives. Over time, these casual interactions evolved into deeper connections. I learned that vulnerability was a strength—by opening up about my struggles as a single parent, I created a space where others felt comfortable sharing their own challenges. This mutual exchange built trust and camaraderie. Church was another sanctuary where I found support. The congregation was welcoming, and I joined a small group that met weekly for prayer and fellowship. These gatherings became a source of spiritual nourishment and emotional encouragement. The women in the group would check on me regularly, often surprising us with meals or offering to babysit when I had an important commitment. Their kindness reminded me that I was not alone on this journey.

The boys' extracurricular activities also became a gateway to building my village. I volunteered to help with events, bake sales, and team fundraisers. Through these activities, I connected with other parents who shared similar values and interests. These relationships extended beyond the events; we began arranging playdates for the kids and coffee meetups for ourselves. Over time, these parents became my allies, always ready to lend a hand when needed. One memorable instance was when I fell ill and couldn't drive the boys to school. Within minutes of sending a group text to a few friends, I had multiple offers to help. One parent picked up the boys and took them to school, another dropped off dinner later that evening, and yet another checked in on me during the day. Moments like these reaffirmed the importance of the community I had built.

Another key aspect of my village was fostering relationships with my neighbors. I made an effort to introduce myself and exchange phone numbers for emergencies. Over time, we developed a rapport, and they became an extension of my support system. Despite the challenges of single parenthood, my village of friendships became a testament to the power of community. It was not just about receiving help; it was about giving back as well. I reciprocated their kindness whenever I could, whether by hosting gatherings, helping with their kids or simply being a listening ear. These acts of reciprocity strengthened our bonds and created a network of mutual support.

Immigrants who are single parents face a unique set of challenges when adjusting to a new culture, but with intentionality and effort, they can not only adapt but thrive. Immersion is key; engaging with local communities, such as schools, places of worship, or community centers, can provide opportunities to meet people and understand cultural norms. Joining parent groups, volunteering, or participating in local events fosters connections and builds a sense of belonging. It's also important to learn and respect the customs and traditions of the new environment while sharing your own culture. This exchange enriches both sides and opens doors for mutual understanding. Building a routine that blends familiar practices with new ones creates a sense of stability for both parent and child. Seeking out resources, such as language classes if that is your case, or immigrant support organizations, can ease the transition and provide practical tools for navigating daily life. Cultivating resilience and maintaining an open mindset allows single parents to turn challenges into opportunities, paving the way for personal growth and a fulfilling life in their new home. By taking deliberate steps to build a village of friendships, I was able to create a nurturing environment for both myself and my boys. The support system I built became my lifeline, enabling me to navigate the challenges of single parenthood with resilience and grace.

Connecting with my African friends was more than just a desire; it was a lifeline to my heritage and a way to maintain a sense of belonging far from home. I was always intentional about meeting people from Ghana or other African countries, as it anchored me to my identity and gave me a sense of community in a foreign land. Every interaction was an opportunity to bridge the gap between my past and my present. One particular moment stands out in my memory. I was teaching a class, and as I took attendance, a name caught my attention: Kwesi. The name resonated deeply with me because it was not just a Ghanaian name but also the name of my son. My heart skipped a beat, and I couldn't help but ask the student, "Are your parents Ghanaian?"

"Yes," he replied, with a smile that felt familiar, as though it carried a shared understanding of who we were and where we came from. I immediately felt a connection and asked him to see me after class. When he approached me, I handed him my phone number and said, "Please give this to your mom. I'd love to meet her."

That small moment of reaching out changed everything. His mother, Aba, did not call me, but we met at the Winter Haven library, and we instantly bonded. Through Aba, I was introduced to a network of Ghanaian families in the area. What started as a simple exchange of numbers grew into a vibrant sisterhood, a community of women who shared not only the same homeland but also the same struggles and joys of navigating life away from it. For me, it was essential to have a balance in my relationships, not just friends who were American and could help me navigate this new world, but also friends from Ghana, who could remind me of the essence of who I was. They were my link to home, and they were my support system. Together, we celebrated our traditions, cooked the foods that reminded us of home, and created a little piece of Ghana in our corner of the world. This sisterhood wasn't just about social gatherings; it was about finding strength and comfort in one another. It was about the stories we shared, the laughter we exchanged, and the shoulders we leaned on during difficult times.

Tips for Building a Support System as a Single Parent

1. Engage with Your Community: Attend school events, church services, and local activities to meet people with shared interests and values.

2. Be Open and Intentional: Authenticity fosters deeper connections and invites others to support you.

3. Volunteer: Get involved in your children's activities or community projects. This not only helps others but also creates opportunities to build relationships.
4. Foster Reciprocity: Offer help when you can. Support systems thrive on mutual give-and-take.
5. Utilize Technology: Create group chats with other parents or neighbors to coordinate support and stay connected.
6. Nurture Relationships: Regularly check in with your friends, neighbors, and support network. Small gestures like a thank you note, or a coffee meetup go a long way.
7. Be Patient: Building a support system takes time. Invest in relationships and allow them to grow naturally.

Chapter Twenty-Four

LEGACY OF LOVE AND LEARNING

"Start children off on the way they should go,
and even when they are old they will not turn from it."
— Proverbs 22:6 (NIV)

A s a single mother, I understood early on that education was the key to unlocking my sons' potential, and I dedicated myself to guiding them every step of the way. When Kwame entered high school, I knew it was time to start preparing for the SAT. After extensive research, I found the University of Central Florida McKnight Achievers program. It offered free ACT and SAT preparation courses and presented the possibility of a full scholarship if the boys decided to attend UCF. Every week, we made the long drive to UCF, knowing the sacrifice of time and energy was worth it. By the time we returned home, it would be late, but we established a rhythm: baths, a quick review of the day's work, and then to bed. The program was invaluable, laying the foundation for Kwame's success.

After Kwame took the PSAT and scored well, college invitations began pouring in. Universities hosted information sessions in Tampa and Orlando, and I took the boys to as many as possible. These sessions were eye-opening, not just for Kwame but for me. As an immigrant, I found the American college system unfamiliar, so I made it a priority to ask questions, particularly about scholarships. I learned that academic excellence, community service, and extracurricular involvement were vital for securing financial aid.

In the summer of his tenth grade, I discovered a study abroad program at Cambridge University in the UK for Kwame. Though the application process was rigorous, involving essays and numerous requirements, we were thrilled when Kwame was accepted. That summer, he had the opportunity to study at one of the world's most prestigious institutions. Meanwhile, Kwesi, who had a keen interest in technology, attended a robotics program at Rollins College. It was a summer of exploration and advancement for both boys and for me, it was a time to take classes needed for my teacher certification.

The following summer was a season of new beginnings and exciting opportunities for both Kwame and Kwesi. Kwame decided to apply to the Ivy Scholars Program at Yale University, a highly competitive summer program designed for high school students who wanted to challenge themselves academically and experience life at an Ivy League school. At the same time, Kwesi continued to deepen his passion for robotics by enrolling in a specialized program at Florida Polytechnic University, where he could build on his knowledge and gain more hands-on experience in engineering and technology.

Before taking Kwame to Yale, we planned a special trip that would take us through some of the colleges in that area. We wanted to visit these schools not just to see their campuses, but to inspire both boys and help them imagine what their future could be. Our journey began with a flight to Boston, a city known for its rich history and world-class universities. The flight was smooth, and as the plane began its descent, I could see the tall buildings and the winding Charles River. I glanced over at the boys, and they were also staring out with excitement. I could feel their anticipation.

Our first stop was Harvard University, one of the most famous schools in the world. The moment we stepped onto campus, I felt the energy of the place. The red brick buildings stood tall and proud, framed by towering trees. Parents and their kids walked around the campus, taking their own tours, eyes wide with curiosity. I think I was the most excited of all. While the boys strolled behind me, taking it all in at their own pace, I was upfront, firing off questions about admissions like I was the one applying.

As we walked through Harvard Yard, I listened as the guide shared stories about the university's long history, its famous alumni, and the traditions that made Harvard unique. Kwame was finally engaged by asking a few questions about student life, academic programs, and the admissions process.

After Harvard, we made our way to the Massachusetts Institute of Technology (MIT), a university known for its groundbreaking research and innovation in science and technology. As soon as we stepped inside one of the engineering buildings, Kwesi's face lit up with excitement. He had always been fascinated by robotics, and MIT's labs were like a dream come true for him. We explored different parts of the campus, visiting the robotics lab, where students were working on advanced projects, and watching some of the robots in action. Kwesi was in his element, absorbing every detail. It was incredible to see him so inspired.

This trip was about more than just seeing famous colleges—it was about showing both boys what was possible for their futures. I wanted them to dream big, to see themselves in these spaces, and to believe that with hard work and dedication, they could achieve anything. We had dinner at a restaurant nearby before going to our hotel to get a good night's rest.

The next day, we drove from Boston to New Haven, Connecticut. The journey was picturesque, with rolling hills and charming New England towns along the way. We stopped for lunch at a quaint diner, sharing laughs and discussing our impressions of the schools we had visited. As we approached Yale's iconic gothic architecture, a sense of awe filled the car. Dropping Kwame off for his summer program was bittersweet; I was proud of his accomplishments but also emotional about leaving him to embark on this new chapter. We hugged tightly, and I reminded him to stay focused and embrace every moment. Before leaving, I met Kwame's roommate and his parents, who were lovely people. Their warmth and friendliness reassured me that Kwame would have good company during his time there.

Kwesi and I returned to Boston to catch our flight back to Florida. The flight home was filled with conversation about the trip. Kwesi, ever curious, asked questions about the colleges and how programs like the ones Kwame was attending could benefit him in the future. Once we landed in Florida, the focus shifted to preparing Kwesi for his summer robotics program at Rollins College in Winter Park. I was relieved to learn that he would be sharing a dorm with the son of a family friend, which brought me great comfort. Moving him into his dorm was an exciting moment; I could see his anticipation as we arranged his belongings and set up his room. After ensuring he was settled, I left feeling proud and optimistic about the summer ahead.

Kwame's senior year was a whirlwind of activity. From retaking the SAT to improve his math scores to managing college applications, we had a structured plan to navigate the process without feeling overwhelmed. I hired a tutor to help him twice a week with math, ensuring his scores reflected his full potential. Despite the hectic schedule filled with prom, senior night, and other activities, we stayed focused on the goal.

When Christmas arrived, we received Kwame's early decision results from Yale: he was deferred. While it was disappointing, we decided to remain hopeful and wait for other admissions decisions. Shortly after the new year, Kwame received an acceptance letter from the University of Florida, and more letters followed. Then, one Friday evening, Kwame asked me to read an email from Cornell University. It read:

Dear Kwame,

You are invited to visit Cornell. This special invitation is extended to you because of your strong academic and personal record and because you will be admitted to Cornell University's Class of 2017.

I couldn't contain my excitement. Kwesi joined us, and together we celebrated with tears and laughter. When Ivy Day arrived, Kwame received a full tuition scholarship to Cornell. It was the culmination of years of sacrifice and hard work. We shared the exciting news with his high school, and the response was incredible! His teachers and the staff members beamed with joy for him. Their faces lit up with pride and excitement as they expressed their heartfelt wishes for his future. I heard that when the announcement was made during chapel, his friends erupted into thunderous applause, their cheers filling the air as they joyously chanted his name.

Parenting Kwame and Kwesi as a single mother taught me resilience and faith. One of the most important lessons I learned as a single mom was the value of resourcefulness. Raising children on a budget required ingenuity in finding free or low-cost programs, applying for scholarships, and leveraging community resources. It also required discipline and organization, from creating schedules that balanced academics and extracurricular activities to setting aside time for family bonding and spiritual growth. Another lesson was the importance of being present. Whether it was attending parent-teacher conferences, cheering from the sidelines at sports events, or driving long hours to educational programs, my presence showed my sons that I believed in them. That belief became the foundation for their confidence and ambition.

Strategic Summer Planning

For single parents looking to maximize their children's summer experiences on a budget, here are some practical tips:

1. Research Free or Low-Cost Programs: Many universities and organizations offer summer programs with scholarships or reduced fees. Start your search early to secure spots in these competitive programs.

2. Leverage Community Resources: Libraries, community centers, and local nonprofits often provide free or affordable activities, from robotics clubs to art workshops.

3. Encourage Volunteering: Community service is not only rewarding but also strengthens college applications. Look for opportunities that align with your child's interests.

4. Create a Learning Schedule: Dedicate time for reading, skill-building, or exploring new hobbies. Online resources and free courses can supplement their education.

5. Plan Affordable Outings: Use summer as an opportunity for experiential learning through trips to museums, parks, or historical sites. Many places offer discounts for students.

6. Set Goals Together: Collaborate with your children to set academic and personal goals for the summer. This fosters accountability and ensures their time is used productively.

Chapter Twenty-Five

THE ROAD TO COLLEGE

"For I know the plans I have for you," declares the Lord,
"plans to prosper you and not to harm you,
plans to give you hope and a future."
— Jeremiah 29:11 (NIV)

Graduation day arrived for Kwame! Mama flew in from Ghana to be with me and the boys. We attended all the awards ceremonies before the festivities. As I sat in the audience watching Kwame walk across the stage to receive his diploma, I was overcome with emotion. Tears flowed freely as the weight of the moment sank in. This was not just a graduation; it was a culmination of years of hard work, perseverance, and faith in God. Our journey had taken us across continents and through numerous challenges, from Germany to Brooklyn and from San Jose to Florida. It was a journey marked by survival and triumph. Some might describe our experiences as an adventure, but for us, it was about finding a way to thrive despite the odds. And here we were, celebrating this incredible milestone. As I looked at Kwame in his cap and gown, I thought about the countless hours of studying, the sacrifices, and the faith it took to get here. Another journey was about to begin as I prepared to send my first child off to college, a new chapter filled with excitement.

We took a trip to Ithaca that summer to tour the campus and the town. We flew into Syracuse and rented a car to Ithaca. The drive from Syracuse to Ithaca was beautiful. Before we left Florida, one of the parents from the boys' school introduced me to a family she knew in Ithaca via email. We emailed each other a couple of times, and I promised to meet them when I was in town.

We fell in love with the Cornell campus right away! The gorges were truly awe-inspiring, with cascading waterfalls that seemed to emerge from a storybook. The combination of towering trees, their leaves whispering in the breeze, and the meticulously maintained lawns created a serene yet vibrant atmosphere. What stood out most was the sense of harmony between the natural beauty and the timeless architecture, making every corner of the campus feel like a perfect blend of history and nature. The tour started at the iconic Arts Quad, a central space surrounded by historic buildings that seemed to whisper the stories of generations of students. The lush greenery and vibrant energy of students walking to and from classes made it feel alive with possibilities. From there, we made our way to the Uris Library, with its towering gothic architecture that seemed to transport us to another era. Inside, the library was equally magnificent, with its grand reading rooms and the smell of old books filling the air. It was easy to imagine hours spent studying or getting lost in its countless volumes.

Next, we visited Sage Chapel, a breathtaking space with intricate stained-glass windows that cast colorful light across the pews. The chapel exuded a sense of serenity and history, and its towering spire added a majestic touch to the campus skyline. Finally, we reached McGraw Tower, which houses the famous Cornell Chimes. The guide shared stories about the tradition of chime concerts, and as we stood there, we could hear the faint echoes of bells in the distance—a truly magical experience. After we toured the campus, we headed to the home of our new friends, who greeted us as though we were old acquaintances. Their warmth and hospitality immediately put us at ease. We spent some time getting to know each other over light refreshments, sharing stories about our journeys and mutual excitement about Cornell. Later, they offered to take us downtown for dinner. The restaurant they chose was cozy and bustling, with delicious aromas wafting through the air. Over dinner, we talked about everything from campus life to local attractions.

Afterward, we leisurely strolled through downtown, admiring the charm of the small shops and cafes illuminated by string lights. We decided to get ice cream, and it felt like the perfect ending to a wonderful day. At the ice cream shop, we struck up a conversation with another couple who turned out to be close friends of our new hosts. They were warm and engaging, and the camaraderie between everyone was infectious. They introduced us and we exchanged phone numbers. Before we left for our hotel, the couple from the ice cream shop casually asked if I had already booked accommodation for move-in day. Initially, I was caught off guard by the question and replied, "Not yet," assuming there was still plenty of time to secure a room.

They then explained how hectic move-in week could be and how hotels in the area quickly filled up. To my surprise, they didn't just offer advice but went a step further, saying, "If you can't find a hotel, let us know. You and your son are more than welcome to stay with us!" I was speechless for a moment, overwhelmed by their generosity. These were people I had just met, extending such a thoughtful and kind gesture. I thanked them sincerely, feeling deeply grateful for their kindness. I was in awe that a couple I just met were willing for my son and me to stay at their house during move-in week because I was already late securing a hotel.

As we sat in the car, driving back to the hotel, I reflected on the day's events. I turned to Kwame and said with a smile, "God is always looking out for us." It felt as though each step of this journey had been carefully guided, from the warm welcome we received to the unexpected offer of help from strangers who already felt like friends. Kwame nodded and said, "I see that, Mom."

We flew back to Florida the next day and began preparing Kwame for college and Kwesi for high school. I knew this was a significant time for all of us, and it became clear to me that it was also time to pursue my dreams. I began researching master's programs for myself. After years of focusing on the boys and ensuring their success, it was time for me to go back to school. The summer came to an end, and Kwesi began ninth grade. Dropping him off at the high school on his first day was a memorable moment. He was so happy and proud to be entering this new chapter of his life, and I was equally proud to see him grow into a confident young man.

The graduation ceremony was beautiful, and I felt a deep sense of gratitude for the friends who came to support us. Their presence was so appreciated. After the celebrations, it was time to focus on getting Kwame ready for college and ensuring Kwesi had a meaningful summer program to attend. The college preparation process was overwhelming. The sheer volume of paperwork was daunting. Navigating the FAFSA application required meticulous attention to detail, and I had to ensure it aligned perfectly with the CSS Profile for the College Board application. Financial terms and processes were new to me, but I was determined to get everything right. I asked countless questions and sought advice whenever I felt unsure.

Before Kwame committed to Cornell, I took the time to call the other schools where he had been accepted. I inquired about their financial aid packages and even negotiated with them to see if they could offer more support. This process required persistence and patience, but I wanted to make sure we explored every option. After carefully reviewing all the offers and considering what was best for Kwame's future, we decided on Cornell. Sending my first child off to college was a bittersweet experience. It marked the beginning of a new journey for him and our family.

Mama stayed with us longer so I could fly Kwame off to college while she stayed with Kwesi in Florida. She reassured me that everything would be fine at home and encouraged me to focus on helping Kwame settle into this new chapter of his life. Kwame had left for Ithaca a couple of weeks earlier to participate in a volunteer program. My new friends in Ithaca had graciously picked him up from the airport and hosted him overnight before he moved to campus. Their kindness eased my mind, as I knew he was in good hands.

When I arrived in Ithaca, I went straight to our new friends' house, where the entire family greeted me warmly. They made me feel at home immediately, offering me a comfortable place to stay and sharing stories about their own experiences with college transitions. Their support was invaluable, and I was deeply grateful for their generosity. I had already made the process much smoother by ordering all the college supplies Kwame needed from Target and other stores and then would be picking them up locally that evening. This small discovery made an overwhelming task much more manageable, and it worked out perfectly for us.

The following morning was a whirlwind of activity as we prepared to move Kwame into his dorm. The excitement and nervous energy were palpable. As we unpacked his belongings and set up his room, I couldn't help but marvel at how far we had come. Once his dorm room was ready, we attended the information sessions for parents. I sat in the auditorium, hanging onto every word the speakers shared about navigating college life and supporting our students from afar. I took copious notes, determined to absorb every detail so that I would be even more prepared when it was Kwesi's turn to embark on this journey. The sessions were both informative and deeply emotional. I thought how quickly time was passing and how much my boys were growing up.

Later that day, we explored the campus together. Kwame pointed out the places he had already discovered during his volunteer program and shared his excitement about the semester ahead. We ended the day with a delightful dinner at one of Cornell's stunning dining halls. The elegant chandeliers cast a warm glow over the beautifully set tables. As we enjoyed our meal, I couldn't help but feel a profound sense of gratitude for all the blessings that had brought us to this moment. After the meal, I returned to my host family's cozy home, and as I crawled into bed, I whispered a prayer of gratitude for all that God had done for me and the boys.

The next day, the college had a gathering of all the new students and their parents at the Schoellkopf Field for convocation. There was a speech and singing the alma mater song and words of encouragement for the new students, and there was a farewell message to parents. I hugged Kwame tightly, praying that God would keep him safe and guide him through this new chapter of his life. We said our goodbyes with tears streaming down our faces.

"I love you so much," he managed to whisper.

"I love you more," I responded, my voice thick with emotion.

Leaving him behind was one of the hardest things I had ever done. But as I walked away, I reminded myself that this was the journey we had chosen. It was a path filled with challenges and sacrifices, but also immense pride and gratitude. Kwame was ready for this new chapter, and so was I.

The drive back to Syracuse was quiet. I didn't play music or turn on the radio. Alone with my thoughts, I suddenly burst into an ugly cry and had to pull over to compose myself. My emotions were raw. Since arriving in the United States, life had been a marathon without a finish line. But in that moment of release, I prayed, calmed myself, and reminded myself to keep going. I couldn't miss my flight back to Florida. When I returned home, mama and Kwesi were happy to see me. I felt a renewed sense of purpose as I promised Kwesi that we would visit his brother during Cornell's parents' weekend.

Strategies for Early College Planning:

1. Start Planning Early
   - Research Schools: Help your child explore colleges early, considering factors like academic programs, location, and financial aid.
   - Understand Application Deadlines: Familiarize yourself with key dates for admissions, FAFSA, and scholarships.
2. Master the Financial Aid Process
   - FAFSA and CSS Profile: Learn the financial aid forms and how to fill them out accurately. Double-check that all financial information matches across documents.
   - Compare Offers: Don't hesitate to contact colleges about financial aid packages. Sometimes you can negotiate for better aid or scholarships.
   - Look for Scholarships: Encourage your child to apply for as many scholarships as possible, even small ones. They do add up!
3. Visit the Campus
   - Schedule Tours: If possible, visit the college campus together. This helps your child visualize life there and feel more comfortable, or you can do virtual tours.

- Explore the Area: Check out the town or city around the campus to understand the environment your child will live in.

4. Organize Dorm Essentials
   - Create a List: Work with your child to list everything they'll need, from bedding to school supplies.
   - Order Ahead: Many stores allow you to shop online and pick up items near the campus, which is especially useful for out-of-state moves.

5. Involve Your Support Network
   - Ask for Help: Don't hesitate to lean on friends or family for advice, assistance, or even moral support.
   - Meet Other Parents: If you can, connect with other parents whose children will be attending the same school. They can be a great resource.

6. Prepare for the Emotional Transition
   - Acknowledge Your Feelings: It's normal to feel a mix of pride, sadness, and anxiety. Give yourself space to process these emotions.
   - Celebrate the Milestone: Focus on the accomplishment and growth this moment represents for both you and your child.

7. Make Move-In Day Special
   - Plan Logistics: Book hotels and plan meals well in advance, as move-in weekends can be hectic.
   - Stay Organized: Bring checklists to ensure nothing important is forgotten.
   - Capture the Moment: Take plenty of photos and enjoy the experience.

8. Build a Communication Plan
   - Set Expectations: Discuss how often you'll check in and what communication methods work best (text, video calls, etc.).
   - Give Them Space: While staying connected is important, also allow your child the freedom to navigate college life independently.
9. Take Care of Yourself
   - Find Your New Routine: With your child off to college, it's a chance to focus on your own goals or hobbies.
   - Celebrate Your Success: Reflect on how far you've come and the role you played in your child's journey.
10. Stay Engaged in Their Journey
    - Visit When Possible: Attend parents' weekends or other campus events to stay involved.
    - Encourage Independence: Offer guidance when needed but let them grow through their experiences.
    - Be Their Cheerleader: Celebrate their accomplishments and remind them of your support.

Chapter Twenty-Six
LETTING GO

"Commit to the Lord whatever you do,
and he will establish your plans."
— Proverbs 16:3 (NIV)

I arrived back in Florida with a profound sense of pride and a renewed commitment to the pursuit of my education. Starting my master's program in school counseling felt like a significant milestone not just for me, but for our entire family. It was a step toward fulfilling a long-held dream, and I approached it with determination. Every other weekend, I made the drive to Tampa for classes, an endeavor that required careful planning and intentionality. Once again, balancing coursework with the responsibilities of being a single parent was challenging, but I was fueled by the belief that this effort would ultimately benefit my family.

At the same time, Kwesi was entering his freshman year of high school, and it was time to begin preparing for college applications. Having gone through this process with Kwame, I felt more prepared to navigate the complexities of applications, essays, and financial aid. Still, each child is unique, and I knew Kwesi's journey would have its own challenges and triumphs. With Kwame now away at college, the house felt quieter, and Kwesi often mentioned how much he missed his brother. Their bond was special, and his absence left a noticeable void. Fortunately, having mama with us provided much-needed stability and comfort. Her presence was a blessing, especially during moments when I felt stretched thin.

Kwesi's high school schedule was packed with activities, and our lives were a whirlwind of events and commitments. Weekends became a delicate balance of my academic pursuits and supporting Kwesi's endeavors. On the weekends when I wasn't attending classes, I made it a priority to be there for him. If he had a lacrosse game, I was on the sidelines, cheering him on with pride. The crisp Florida afternoons were often filled with the sounds of whistles and cheers, and I loved seeing Kwesi in his element, playing with such passion and focus.

On the days when he didn't have a game, we established a cherished routine. We would start our mornings with breakfast at one of our favorite local diners. Over breakfast, we shared conversations about his plans, dreams, and the challenges he faced. These moments were precious a chance to connect amid our busy schedules. After breakfast, we headed to the Winter Haven library, a place that had become our sanctuary of productivity. Kwesi worked diligently on his assignments, researching colleges and drafting essays, while I focused on my coursework. I wanted Kwesi to know that I believed in him and that, just as I had supported his brother, I was fully committed to helping him achieve his goals. But our weekends weren't all work and no play. I understood the importance of allowing Kwesi to relax and enjoy his teenage years. We made time to visit friends, play games, and simply have fun. I wanted him to feel that he wasn't missing out on the joys of life, even as we worked hard to prepare for his future.

Cornell's Parent Weekend came around, and I flew to Ithaca with Kwesi to spend time with Kwame. The crisp autumn air greeted us as we landed, and the vibrant foliage painted the campus in shades of gold, orange, and red. It was my first visit back to Ithaca since dropping Kwame off, and I couldn't wait to see how he was settling in. Kwesi was equally excited, eager to reconnect with his brother and experience a glimpse of college life. When Kwame met us at the entrance to his dorm, his wide smile and confident demeanor reassured me that he was adjusting well to his new environment. He had lost weight and was more self-assured, and there was a spark of independence in his eyes. We hugged tightly, and I couldn't help but feel a rush of pride seeing the young man he was becoming. We spent the weekend immersed in campus life. Cornell had planned a series of events for parents, including tours, faculty lectures, and a special reception. Kwesi was fascinated by the sprawling campus, especially the clock tower and its famous chimes. Kwame gave us a tour, proudly showing off the library where he studied, the dining hall where he ate, and the scenic spots he had discovered, including a peaceful overlook of Cayuga Lake.

One of the highlights of the weekend was a family brunch hosted in one of the grand dining halls. The tables were adorned with fresh flowers, and the spread of food was impressive: freshly baked pastries, omelets made to order, and local apple cider. That evening, we attended a Cornell football game at Schoellkopf Field. The energy in the stadium was electric, with students and families cheering loudly. Kwesi was in awe of the camaraderie and school spirit. Kwame explained the traditions, laughing as he recounted his own experiences of adjusting to campus culture. After the game, we decided to keep things simple and have dinner at a cozy pizzeria in College Town.

Later that night, back in our hotel room, Kwesi and I stayed up late talking about the future. He admitted that seeing Kwame thrive at Cornell had inspired him. "I want to find a school where I can grow like Kwame is," he said earnestly.

Sunday came too quickly, and it was time to say goodbye. As we stood outside Kwame's dorm, I hugged him tightly, feeling the familiar mix of pride and longing. "Keep working hard and take care of yourself," I said, my voice thick with emotion. "I will, Mom," he replied with a smile. Kwesi gave his brother a firm handshake before pulling him into a hug. "See you at Christmas," Kwesi said, trying to sound casual but emotional. As Kwesi and I walked back to the car, I looked back one last time to see Kwame waving goodbye. The weekend was beautiful, and we were grateful to have participated in Cornell's parents' weekend.

On the flight back to Florida, Kwesi rested his head on my shoulder and dozed off, exhausted from the weekend's excitement. I stared out the window at the clouds, whispering a silent prayer of gratitude for the journey we were on.

Time seemed to move at lightning speed. Before I knew it, the first year of high school and college had flown by. That summer, both boys continued their respective programs. Kwame began taking on internships to gain professional experience, while Kwesi participated in various summer programs to strengthen his college applications. Kwame returned home for the summer, planning to unwind for a week before starting his internship in D.C. I decided to drive Kwame to Washington, D.C., for his summer internship so I leased an SUV, and the three of us embarked on a 16-hour road trip. The drive was long, but the time spent together was priceless. We listened to music I did not care for, but I sang along anyway. Once we arrived in D.C., we helped Kwame settle into his room. Afterward, Kwesi and I explored the city, visiting landmarks and enjoying the vibrant atmosphere of D.C.

On our way back to Florida, we made a stop in South Carolina to visit a friend, which added another layer of warmth and connection to our journey. A couple of days after we arrived in Florida, I prepared Kwesi for his flight to Connecticut for his summer program. I dropped him off at the airport, carefully going over the rules for navigating airports on his own and finding the van that would take him to campus. It was important to me that my boys learned to be independent. Sending Kwame to Cambridge by himself at age 14 had been a challenge, but he had mastered the skill of traveling alone. Now, it was Kwesi's turn to take that step.

As Kwesi's junior year began, spring break presented another opportunity to focus on his preparation for college. I enrolled him in an intensive SAT program at Rollins College. Every morning, we made the hour-and-a-half drive to the campus. While he attended classes, I used the time to study at the local library or take walks to clear my mind. Kwesi wasn't thrilled about missing out on beach trips with his friends, and seeing their Snapchat stories only made it harder for him. I reminded him that we couldn't afford the luxury of distractions. Sacrifices were necessary to achieve the goals we had set for ourselves. The college application process for Kwesi was officially underway.

Around the same time, Kwame returned home to take the LSAT. He chose to sit for the exam at Barry University in Orlando, and I took the day off to accompany him. Before he entered the exam hall, I prayed with him, asking for focus and clarity. While he took the test, I struck up a conversation with another parent in the waiting area. We exchanged stories about our journeys as parents, finding comfort in the shared experience. After three hours, the exam was over, and Kwame emerged with a sense of relief. We celebrated by stopping for lunch before making our way back to Winter Haven.

That summer marked another milestone for me: I graduated with my master's degree in school counseling. Shortly afterward, I took my school counseling certification exams, ready to embark on a new chapter in my professional life. A fresh journey awaited me in the fall as I began my doctoral studies.

Plan for Searching for Internships and Summer Programs Early in the Year

Set Clear Goals

- Define Your Interests: Identify industries, fields, or skills you want to explore.

- Set Objectives: Determine whether you want to gain hands-on experience, build your network, or develop specific skills.

Develop a Timeline
- January-February: Begin your search for opportunities. Many summer programs and internships have deadlines between February and April.
- March-April: Finalize and submit applications.
- May-June: Prepare for interviews and accept offers.

Research Opportunities
- Online Platforms: Use websites like Indeed, LinkedIn, Handshake, and Glassdoor.
- Professional Associations: Program listings or internship postings.
- Local Opportunities: Research community organizations and nonprofits in your state.

Build Your Application Materials
- Resume: Update with your latest experience, emphasizing relevant skills.
- Cover Letter: Customize for each application, highlighting your fit for the role.
- References: Contact previous employers or mentors to confirm their willingness to support you.

Network Strategically
- Leverage Connections: Talk to other students, friends, and career office.

- Attend Events: Join career fairs, webinars, or local networking events.
- Follow-Up: After meetings or applications, send thank you notes and keep in touch.

Prepare for Applications

- Track Deadlines: Use a spreadsheet or app to keep track of opportunities, deadlines, and application status.
- Practice Interviews: Prepare answers to common questions and rehearse with friends or colleagues.
- Gather Materials: Have your transcripts, recommendation letters, and writing samples ready.

Explore Alternatives

- Online Courses: Consider enrolling in short-term courses to boost your qualifications.
- Volunteer Work: Look for ways to gain experience if internships are competitive.
- Independent Projects: Plan personal projects or research to build your portfolio.

Evaluate and Follow Up

- Review Offers: Compare program details like pay, location, and professional development opportunities.
- Send Thank You Notes: After interviews or receiving offers, express your gratitude.
- Reflect: At the end of the summer, assess what you learned and update your resume.

Chapter Twenty-Seven

A SEASON OF PREPARATION
AND PROMISE

*"Commit to the Lord whatever you do, and He
will establish your plans."*
— *Proverbs 16:3 (NIV)*

The boys' senior year was a whirlwind of excitement and endless planning. Kwame was finishing his final year of college, while Kwesi was wrapping up his high school journey. It was a monumental time for our family, filled with anticipation and the culmination of years of hard work. When Kwame's LSAT results arrived, we could barely contain our excitement. He had scored exceptionally well, opening the doors to virtually any law school he wished to attend. Meanwhile, Kwesi had set his sights on colleges in the Boston area, eager to carve his own path. While Kwame worked on law school applications, Kwesi was busy with college applications and a packed senior year. Kwesi's accomplishments brought their share of joy, with his active involvement in school activities earning him nominations for prestigious awards, including the Silver Garland Award.

As the first semester of his senior year ended, Kwame returned home for the holidays. It was a joyful reunion, and he didn't waste any time lending his expertise to help Kwesi complete his college applications. Soon after, the acceptance letters started rolling in. Law schools began calling Kwame, congratulating him, and offering not only admissions but generous financial awards. Each call and letter was met with celebrations, but one morning brought news that surpassed all our expectations. Kwesi and I were on our way to a dental appointment when Kwame called us, his voice barely able to contain his excitement. "Mom, Kwesi, you won't believe it!" he exclaimed. "Harvard Law School just called. They've accepted me with a financial award!" The car erupted in cheers. Kwesi and I couldn't wait to get home and share the joyous moment with Kwame. That Christmas was one of the happiest we'd ever experienced; we were grateful for what lay ahead.

The new year rolled in with an avalanche of acceptance letters for Kwesi. Each one was celebrated, but there was one school he was eagerly waiting to hear from: Boston University. One evening, just before a planned trip to Boston for Harvard Law's admitted students' weekend, Kwesi went out to the movies with friends. He returned home with the news we'd been waiting for. Boston University had sent an email confirming his acceptance, along with a Presidential Scholarship that covered both tuition and room and board. I dropped to my knees, overwhelmed with gratitude, praising God for His goodness. Kwesi immediately called Kwame to share the news, and the joy in his voice was palpable. Knowing that the two brothers would be in the same city added more happiness to an amazing moment. The timing was perfect as we prepared to visit Boston.

Arriving in Boston, Kwesi and I took an Uber straight to Harvard's campus. As we stepped out of the car and walked toward the law school, I felt a wave of emotions wash over me. Memories of late-night study sessions, countless trips to the library, and the endless miles I'd driven to support their activities all came flooding back. It was as though everything we had endured was crystallizing into this moment of triumph. I was filled with pride and gratitude.

At the registration desk, we received our gift bags and name tags. When the lady at the desk asked for our student's name, her face lit up upon hearing Kwame's. "Oh, I met him yesterday," she said warmly. "We are so excited to have him here at Harvard Law." Her enthusiasm made the experience even more surreal. We met up with Kwame and attended the events planned for admitted students. The sessions were inspiring, and the energy of the campus was infectious.

Later, we took an Uber to Boston University to tour the campus. Boston University's campus was stunning, with its mix of historic buildings and modern facilities nestled along the Charles River. Kwesi was captivated by the vibrant atmosphere, and the view of the river added an extra beauty. We strolled through the campus, exploring the library, dormitories, and student union. Every corner seemed to buzz with energy and possibilities. As we stood on the steps of one of the main buildings, Kwesi turned to me, his face glowing with excitement. "This is it, Mom. I can see myself here." His confidence filled me with pride, and I knew this was the right place for him. The proximity of the two schools was a delightful surprise, and I turned to Kwesi and said, "My baby is going to college." Kwesi rolled his eyes, laughing. "Mom, you already have a son finishing college." We all burst into laughter!

Our time in Boston flew by, but the memories we made were unforgettable. Kwame returned to Ithaca to finish his final semester, while Kwesi and I headed back to Florida to complete his senior year. As the plane ascended into the sky, I reclined my head with tears streaming down my face, aware that the journey had been difficult; nevertheless, every sacrifice, every sleepless night, and every tear had been worthwhile.

Senior year was wrapping up for both boys, and I also began my doctoral studies journey amid their busiest year. It was a whirlwind of activities, balancing my coursework and their senior milestones. The days were filled with preparations for two graduations. each a significant milestone marking the culmination of years of hard work. Kwesi's commencement came first, a week before Kwame's. Kwame made the trip to be there for his brother. The ceremony was held in the beautiful Branscomb auditorium, packed with proud families and friends. When Kwesi's name was called, he walked confidently to the microphone as one of the student speakers. My heart swelled with pride, and I couldn't hold back tears. As he spoke, his words resonated with the journey we had taken. I silently thanked God for the grace that had brought us this far. Kwesi walked across the stage to receive his diploma, and we clapped and shouted his name so loudly that heads turned. It was truly a proud moment. After the ceremony, we joined friends to celebrate, laugh, and share memories. Kwame flew back to Ithaca the next day, but the joy of the occasion lingered as Kwesi and I began preparing for the next big event, Kwame's graduation.

Later that week, Kwesi and I were set to fly to Syracuse and then drive to Ithaca for Kwame's commencement. We arrived at Orlando International Airport full of excitement, ready for the journey. However, things quickly took a turn. An announcement came over the intercom that our flight was delayed. Initially, I remained optimistic, thinking we'd still make it in time. But as the hours dragged on, the delay extended until, at 4:00 a.m., the flight was canceled. Exhausted and frustrated, I went to the counter with tears in my eyes, pleading with the airline representative to find a solution. The man at the counter saw my desperation and assured me he would do everything to get us to New York. He found a flight to JFK leaving within the hour and arranged for us to board. Without our luggage, Kwesi and I rushed to the gate, and the gate attendant ushered us into the plane. As we settled into our seats, I whispered a prayer of gratitude.

At JFK, we learned there were no flights to Syracuse but managed to secure tickets to Buffalo. My mind raced as I worked to adjust our car rental reservation. Once in Buffalo, we filed a claim for our luggage, picked up the rental car, and began the drive to Ithaca. Kwesi fell asleep almost immediately, and I kept myself awake with gospel music and brief stops to rest. By the grace of God, we arrived safely in Ithaca, where Kwame was waiting to greet us. The weekend was a joyous reunion. My uncle and his family came from Canada, and Auntie Judy and Uncle Richie joined us from Brooklyn. Though our luggage didn't arrive until Saturday morning, it didn't dampen our spirits. The celebrations began Friday night with family dinners and heartfelt conversations.

Sunday morning brought the highlight of the weekend: Kwame's commencement. The excitement in the air was palpable as we woke up early, eager to witness this monumental occasion. The house buzzed with activity as we hurried to get dressed, double-checking cameras and phones to capture every special moment. We stepped outside to a crisp morning, the energy of graduation day crackling all around us. As we made our way to Schoellkopf Field, we joined a steady stream of proud families and friends, all heading toward the stadium with smiles and a sense of triumph in the air. The closer we got, the more the anticipation built. This was the moment we had all been waiting for.

As Kwame marched in with his class, he spotted us in the crowd and waved. We cheered enthusiastically, our voices joining the sea of celebration. The president conferred degrees upon the graduates, and the moment arrived when they moved their tassels from right to left, a symbolic act marking their achievement. Caps flew into the air, and Schoellkopf Field erupted in applause. Though Cornell did not call students to the stage individually, tents were set up across the campus for each major to celebrate. We joined Kwame at his department's tent, where professors and students mingled, sharing stories and expressing gratitude. We posed for pictures and hugged one another, and we were all overwhelmed with joy.

We celebrated at one of the restaurants on Cayuga Lake, where the evening was filled with laughter, clinking glasses, and joyful conversations. The restaurant bustled with families toasting to their graduates. It felt like one grand Cornell family celebration, bound together by pride and achievement. We indulged in delicious food, shared memories, and raised our glasses to Kwame's success, soaking in the beauty of the lake under the soft glow of the setting sun. By the time we left the restaurant, the night had stretched late, but our hearts were full. The next morning, reality set in as we headed to Kwame's apartment to help him sort, clean, and pack his belongings. The space that had been his home in his senior year, filled with books, keepsakes, and remnants of his journey, now had to be emptied. As we filled the boxes with his belongings, nostalgia washed over us, flooding our minds with memories of his time at Cornell—the friendships forged, the hurdles he overcame, and the personal growth he experienced. Yet, as an African mom, a nagging instinct compelled me to inquire about the items I had painstakingly purchased for him, only to learn that many had been lost or given away. His dismissive responses made me pause; perhaps it was best to let go of these questions and instead shift the atmosphere to something lighter, bantering and sharing laughs as the final chapter of this journey came to a close. Finally, with the last box sealed and the apartment clean, we said goodbye to Kwame, who was going to stay a few more weeks in Ithaca with friends. Kwame's graduation came to an end and a new chapter of his educational journey awaited.

Chapter Twenty-Eight

A BATTLE FOR MY LIFE AND THEIRS

"Praise the Lord, my soul, and forget not all his benefits—
who forgives all your sins and heals all your diseases."
— Psalm 103:2 -3 (NIV)

Summer began with Kwame traveling to DC for a summer job at the DC Appeals Court while Kwesi took the summer to get ready for college. I decided to catch my breath and take care of myself. I scheduled my mammogram and bloodwork, thinking little of it beyond routine self-care. After my mammogram, I was asked to retake images and undergo an ultrasound. The radiologist mentioned some differences from my last exam and suggested a biopsy. Though slightly concerned, I reminded myself that knowledge is power, and I scheduled the procedure.

A couple of weeks later, my physician's assistant called, mentioning that my biopsy results were in, but my doctor was on vacation. She offered to share the results, or I could wait. I chose to know.

Kwesi accompanied me to the appointment. My heart pounded as we waited, my breath uneven with anxiety. When the PA entered, her face was grim. She asked if I wanted Kwesi to stay. I nodded. Then she said it: "You have cancer."

The words stopped in time. I couldn't breathe. I couldn't think. I was suspended in a surreal reality. Kwesi touched my arm. "Mom." His voice grounded me, and I turned to meet his eyes, brimming with determination. "Mom, you are going to be okay."

I gathered myself. "What stage?" I managed to ask.

"You have Ductal Carcinoma In Situ: stage zero."

Kwesi exhaled deeply. "Thank God! Mom, you are going to be okay."

Kwesi and I sat in the car, the weight of the news settling over us like a thick fog. Tears streamed down my face as I stared out of the windshield, my mind blank yet racing at the same time. Kwesi reached over and held my hand. "Mom, you're going to be okay," he whispered, his voice steady despite the fear I knew he must have been feeling.

We both knew there was one more person we needed to tell. Kwame was in DC, hours away, unaware that our world had just shifted. I took a deep breath and dialed his number, my hands trembling as I held the phone to my ear. The moment he answered, I could hear the joy in his voice. "Hey, Mom! How did the appointment go?"

I tried to respond, but the words wouldn't come. The lump in my throat was too thick, the pain too raw. Kwesi took the phone from me and said, "Kwame, Mom has cancer."

There was silence on the other end—heavy, suffocating silence. Then a sharp inhale. "What?" His voice cracked. I could hear him struggling to process the words, just as I had minutes earlier. "What kind of cancer? What did the doctor say?"

I took the phone back, wiping my tears. "It's stage zero, Ductal Carcinoma In Situ," I explained, my voice barely above a whisper. "The doctor said it's non-invasive. They caught it early."

Kwame exhaled, the tension in his voice giving way to determination. "Mom, you are going to beat this. You're the strongest person I know. You've overcome so much; you're going to get through this too."

His steady belief in me cracked something open inside. I wanted to believe him, but in that moment, all I felt was fear. We talked a little longer before hanging up, but I knew Kwame was shaken. My boys had already endured so much with me. I hated that I was adding another burden to their hearts.

The drive home was silent. I couldn't process my thoughts; they twisted and turned, demanding answers I didn't have. I was angry at God. I had spent years fighting to create a stable life, working tirelessly to raise my boys, and to give them every opportunity I could. And now, just as I was starting to exhale, this? Why now? Why me?

When we got home, I sat at the kitchen table and made a list of the close friends and family members I needed to call. Each name felt like another weight on my chest. How do you tell people something like this? How do you say, "I have cancer" without it feeling like you're breaking their hearts?

I took a week to cry and pray. At night, my pillow was soaked with tears, silent sobs wracking my body as I wrestled with fear, anger, and disbelief. Even though I was mad at God, I needed Him more than ever. I begged for strength, for peace, for the courage to face what lay ahead.

Slowly, I began making the calls. Each conversation was met with shock, sadness, and an outpouring of love. My village, as I call them, was ready to fight alongside me. One of my close friends, whose husband was a medical doctor, wasted no time. He immediately set up an appointment for me with one of the top breast surgeons in our county. I decided not to tell most of my family members yet. They lived so far away, and I didn't want them to worry, especially when I didn't even have all the answers myself. But there was one person I knew I could count on, and that was my friend Connie.

Connie and I met while taking a Family Psychology course, and we had been inseparable ever since. She is one of the most selfless people I've known, and the moment she heard the news, she dropped everything to be by my side. "You are not doing this alone," she told me firmly. "We're in this together."

On the day of my appointment with the surgeon, Connie and another dear friend, Mariela, came with me. They took notes, asked questions, and held space for me when my mind couldn't keep up with everything the doctor was saying. I was still trying to process what was happening to me, but with them by my side, I felt a little less alone.

Now, it was time to fight. But this time, the battle wasn't about survival in a new country, raising my boys alone, or finding a way to provide. This battle was for my health, for my future, for the life I had worked so hard to build. And I was ready.

My sister friends, whom I affectionately refer to as my village, joined together to form a powerful prayer chain that enveloped me in support. Each morning, my uncle uplifted my spirit by sending me heartfelt scriptures and affirmations that filled my heart with hope and courage. Meanwhile, Kwame returned home earlier than expected, eager to be by my side and support both me and Kwesi during this challenging time. Though my schedule was packed with medical appointments in preparation for my upcoming surgery, my priority remained to get Kwesi ready for his college journey. After a heartfelt discussion with my surgeon, we set the date for my surgery a month later, allowing me the much-needed time to travel and help Kwesi move into his dormitory. Just like Kwame's freshman year at Cornell, Kwesi had also been accepted into an enriching summer bridge program that offered him the unique opportunity to arrive on campus two weeks in advance. This early arrival would not only help him acclimate to college life but also foster new friendships and give him a vital head start on his academics before the bustling official move-in day arrived.

Kwame, ever the steadfast and protective older brother, resolved to accompany Kwesi on his journey to Boston. Despite facing his own significant transition embarking on the rigorous path of law school at Harvard, he felt compelled to ensure that his younger sibling had the support he needed to settle into his new program.

I felt relieved knowing that Kwesi would have his big brother around to support him during those important weeks. Two weeks later, I boarded a flight to Boston, my heart heavy with the burden of my recent diagnosis but equally determined to be present for Kwesi during this pivotal moment. Stepping onto the BU campus brought back a rush of feelings of pride mixed with some bittersweet memories, kind of like the day I helped Kwame move into his dorm years ago. You could feel the buzz of new beginnings in the air, but there was also that sense of reality setting in about the challenges to come.

Kwesi greeted me with a wide smile, eager to show me around his new world. We spent the day navigating campus, meeting his roommates, and making countless trips to Target and Bed, Bath & Beyond, ensuring his dorm had everything he needed. I watched as he carefully arranged his books, folded his clothes into his drawers, and set up his workspace, marveling at how my baby boy had suddenly become a young man.

I was determined to carve out some quality time for Kwame during this significant transition in his life. He had just settled into his dorm at Harvard Law School, a place steeped in history and prestige. The ride to Cambridge was filled with anticipation, and as we walked through the iconic Harvard Yard, I could see the warmth of his excitement mingling with a hint of nervous anticipation in his eyes. He happily showed me around the yard, highlighting the spots that had become significant in his life. We talked about his classes, his professors, and his goals. I could see how much he had grown not just in intellect but in confidence. This was the next step in his dream, and I was grateful that I got to witness it.

Throughout my time in Boston, I split my days between both boys, making sure they each felt my presence, my love, and my support. We shared meals together, laughed over old memories, and made new ones. Though I carried the silent burden of my diagnosis, I refused to let it overshadow these precious moments. My boys needed to know that they still had my full attention, just as they always had.

On my last night before flying back to Florida, we had dinner together—just the three of us. As we sat at the table, the conversation drifted from childhood memories to their hopes for the future. I watched them, soaking in their laughter, their banter, their bond.

Then, as we stood outside the restaurant, the time came to say goodbye. They both pulled me into a tight embrace, holding on longer than usual.

"You're going to be okay, Mom," Kwesi whispered.

Kwame nodded, his voice steady. "Mom, you've always been the strongest person we know. You've got this."

I held them tighter, drawing strength from their belief in me.

As I boarded my flight the next morning, I took one last look at the city below. My boys were stepping into their futures, and I was stepping into my battle.

I arrived in Florida ready for war.

Worship music filled my mornings. My anthem was "Good, Good Father" by Chris Tomlin, a reminder of faith amid fear. My village of friends surrounded me with prayers, love, and encouragement.

The night before my surgery, Connie moved in with me. She created a group chat to keep everyone informed. On the morning of my surgery, Chris, Mariela, and Kelly joined Connie at the hospital. My surgeon, sensing my anxiety, offered a prayer. My uncle called with a blessing. The anesthesiologist distracted me with jokes. Then, I fell asleep.

When I awoke, the pain was intense, but so was the love surrounding me. Connie took me home, where the next days were focused on healing. Then came an unexpected complication—Hurricane Irma. Connie's family took us in as we hunkered down together, a storm outside mirroring the storm inside.

A week later, at my post-op appointment, my surgeon walked in with a radiant smile. "I have good news, Vivian. You are cancer-free."

I exhaled the breath I didn't realize I had been holding. Every test was negative. No cancer remained.

Tears streamed down my face. Connie cried too. We hugged, overwhelmed by gratitude. The doctor reminded me that while I was cancer-free, I still needed radiation. Healing wasn't just a one-time event; it was a journey.

Returning to work after a month of sick leave felt like stepping into a familiar world with new eyes. My responsibilities were lighter, and my colleagues welcomed me back with warmth and concern. But as I settled into my routine, another battle loomed ahead: radiation therapy. Thirty-five rounds. That was the number. It sounded daunting when my doctor first told me, but I knew this was the next step in my healing. The treatments would take place every weekday, and after much thought, I decided to schedule them in the evenings. I wanted to keep my energy up during the workday and avoid starting each morning with the weight of treatment on my shoulders.

The drive to the radiation center was a quiet one, forty-five minutes each way. Most of my friends had their own obligations, and while they offered to accompany me, I often found myself declining. Deep down, I think I needed that solitude. In those silent drives, I spoke to God, pouring out my fears, my gratitude, and my determination to come out of this stronger. The first day at the center, I stepped into a waiting room filled with women who, like me, were on their own journeys. Some had lost their hair, their scarves wrapped gently around their heads like crowns of resilience. Others looked weary, their bodies showing signs of the battle they had been fighting for far too long. Yet, despite the exhaustion in their eyes, there was strength, a quiet, steadfast determination to keep going. I checked in at the front desk, where the receptionists greeted me with a kindness that felt almost sacred in that space. They handed me a gown, and I was ushered to a changing area before meeting with the radiologist.

I had so many questions: why 35 rounds? Was it truly necessary? Would I feel weaker as time went on? The radiologist, a patient and empathetic woman, took her time explaining everything. She reassured me that while it was a long process, each session was crucial in reducing the risk of recurrence.

The treatment itself was brief but relentless. I lay on a cold table as a large machine rotated above me, humming softly, directing invisible beams of energy at my body. The first few sessions felt surreal, but soon, the side effects set in. My skin darkened and burned, the tenderness growing with each passing week. The fatigue was unlike anything I had ever known bone-deep, unshakable, an exhaustion that no amount of sleep could cure.

Driving home became a battle in itself. Some days, I pulled over, gripping the steering wheel, waiting for a wave of dizziness to pass. Other days, I arrived home and collapsed onto the couch, unable to do anything but close my eyes and breathe through the discomfort.

One afternoon, I again asked my radiologist why so many treatments were necessary. "Because we want to be sure," she said gently. "We're not just treating what we see. We're treating what we can't." I nodded, absorbing her words. This was not just about the cancer I had; it was about ensuring it never returned.

Through it all, my village held me up. Connie coordinated meals and check-ins. All my sister friends sent messages of encouragement. Kwame and Kwesi called daily, their voices a lifeline on the hardest days. I clung to my faith, to the worship songs that had become my armor. And slowly, the days ticked by.

Then came the final day.

I walked into the treatment center, my body weary, my spirit tested, but my heart full of determination. When the last session ended, a nurse smiled and gestured toward the bell mounted on the wall. "It's time," she said. I hadn't thought much about this moment, but as I reached for the rope, emotion swelled within me.

I hesitated, staring at it. The bell was more than a symbol. It was a victory cry after months of uncertainty, pain, and perseverance. I reached for the rope, took a deep breath, and rang it.

The sound echoed through the room, loud and clear.

Tears filled my eyes. Around me, nurses and patients clapped. I wasn't just finishing treatment. I was stepping into a new chapter. A chapter where I faced cancer and won.

Healing is a process. Though I rang that bell, I knew my health would require continued care.

I whispered a quiet prayer, thanking God for carrying me through and thanking Him for my medical team, the friends who had checked in on me, and the family who had stood by my side. I thought of my boys, Kwame and Kwesi, who would soon be home for the Christmas holidays.

I was still here. I was still standing. And when they came home for Christmas, I would greet them not as a woman consumed by illness, but as their strong, resilient mother, whole, healed, and ready to embrace life.

A Final Thought: Taking Your Health Seriously

My journey taught me invaluable lessons about health, faith, and resilience. I urge every woman reading this to prioritize her well-being.

- When was your last mammogram?
- Do you know your family history of breast cancer?
- Are you familiar with the signs of breast cancer and the importance of early detection?
- Have you had a conversation with your doctor about breast density and additional screenings?
- What steps are you taking to prioritize self-care and wellness?

Your health is your greatest wealth. Don't wait! Take action today.

Chapter Twenty-Nine
RESTORED

"And after you have suffered a little while, the God of all grace, who has called you to His eternal glory in Christ, will Himself restore, confirm, strengthen, and establish you."
—1 Peter 5:10 (ESV)

In March of 2020, the world as we knew it came to a sudden and unimaginable halt. The COVID-19 pandemic swept across the globe, bringing with it fear, uncertainty, and grief. Life was no longer predictable. The things we once took for granted, simple outings, seeing loved ones, walking into a classroom or office, became impossible overnight. I was in the final stretch of my doctoral journey, the very summit of a climb that had taken years of faith, sacrifice, and late-night study sessions. Kwame was also nearing the finish line, his final year of law school. And Kwesi, my baby, was deep in the whirlwind of his junior year at Boston University, immersed in projects and papers for his degree in Architectural Design.

When the nation shut down, the boys came home. And suddenly, we were back under one roof. What could have been a season of overwhelming fear and chaos became, for us, a sacred pause. We cooked together, worked from different corners of the house, encouraged one another through Zoom fatigue and endless updates, and even rediscovered the joy of simply being in each other's presence. In a world turned upside down, we had the gift of togetherness. I remember the day I defended my dissertation virtually. My heart was pounding as I sat before a panel, camera on, notes beside me. But behind the screen, just out of view, were my sons—cheering me on, praying, and holding space for me. When I was told I had passed, tears spilled down my cheeks. I wasn't just earning a doctorate; I was standing on the other side of years of hardship, heartache, and healing.

Shortly after, Kwame completed his Juris Doctor. His graduation was held on Zoom, a format that once felt distant but, in this moment, brought us all closer. We invited family and friends from near and far to watch the commencement live. Faces from across the country—and even the world—filled the screen. Grandparents, aunts, uncles, cousins, childhood friends, and mentors all showed up virtually, clapping, smiling, and cheering from their homes. It was truly a beautiful moment. People who would not have been able to attend in person under normal circumstances were able to celebrate this achievement with us in real time. Though we weren't in a grand auditorium, the love, pride, and joy in that virtual space was overwhelming. It was a beautiful ceremony, and an unforgettable memory.

In 2021, Kwesi also crossed the finish line, graduating with his degree in Architectural Design. This time, Kwame and I made the trip to Boston to support him. Due to social distancing protocols, we weren't allowed into the stadium for the ceremony. Instead, like many other proud parents, we gathered at a nearby restaurant just outside the stadium to watch it unfold. The atmosphere was electric as parents huddled together, cheering on their children, eyes fixed on the screens as their names were called. When Kwesi's name was announced, I clapped with everything in me. Though we weren't inside the stadium, we were right where we needed to be, close enough to feel the joy, to witness the moment, and to celebrate this incredible milestone.

That evening, we celebrated at the Boston Seaport. The sun dipped low over the water, casting a golden glow on the harbor, and my heart was full. As we laughed, ate, and reflected on the journey that had brought us there, I couldn't help but marvel at how far we had come. From a tiny apartment in Brooklyn to living paycheck to paycheck in California to the long drives, the tears, the prayers, and now, this. Restoration didn't come all at once. It came in layers, over the years, in small victories and sacred milestones. And now here we were, standing tall in a moment we once only dreamed of. Today, my sons are "adulting," as they say. Independent. Bold. Kind. Vision-driven. I am now the mother of two grown men. And while our dinner table conversations have shifted from schoolwork and cartoons to legal briefs and design stories, the love between us has only deepened. I marvel at who they've become, not just for their accomplishments, but for the men of integrity, compassion, and resilience they are.

As for me? I'm still becoming. Still growing, learning how to rest. Still finding joy in mentoring, teaching, leading, dancing, traveling, and dreaming new dreams. I've learned that restoration doesn't mean going back to who I was before the pain. It means moving forward with strength I didn't know I had. If you've walked this journey with me through these pages, I want you to know this: Your story isn't over. Whether you are in a season of loss, rebuilding, or rising, there is more ahead. More joy. More healing. More purpose. You, too, can be restored.

I once stood in the ashes of a life that felt broken beyond repair. But Grace picked me up. Grit kept me going. And Growth transformed me.

I am no longer the woman who walked through divorce, poverty, shame, and heartache. I am a woman restored, by faith, by love, by the firm belief that God was not finished with me yet.

And He's not finished with you either.

EPILOGUE

As I reflect on this journey, I am filled with profound gratitude. Life has tested me in ways I never imagined, yet each trial has shaped the person I am today. From navigating single parenthood in a new country to battling cancer with steadfast faith, every challenge became a testament to resilience, hope, and love. The day I rang the bell at the radiation center marked the end of one battle, but it also signaled the beginning of a new chapter. Healing is not a destination; it is a continuous process that requires care, intention, and grace. My story is not just about survival but about embracing life with all its uncertainties, finding strength in vulnerability, and holding onto faith even when the path is unclear.

As I watched my boys grow into remarkable young men, I found renewed purpose. Kwame and Kwesi became my anchor, my reason to keep pushing forward. Their belief in me, even in my weakest moments, was the light that guided me through the darkest times. They taught me that love transcends fear, and hope is the most potent antidote to despair.

This book is not just a recollection of my past; it is a tribute to every woman who has faced adversity with courage, every mother who has sacrificed for her children, and every individual who has fought for their dreams against all odds. It is a reminder that our stories matter, our voices deserve to be heard, and our lives are meant to inspire.

To those who have walked this journey with me, my family, friends, and my steadfast village, thank you. Your prayers, support, and love carried me when my strength faltered. To the medical professionals who cared for me with compassion and expertise, I am eternally grateful.

As I close this chapter, I look ahead with hope. There will be more challenges, more lessons, and more triumphs. But with faith, love, and resilience, I am ready for whatever comes next.

And to you, dear reader, may my story remind you that no matter how difficult the journey is, you are never alone. Keep believing, keep fighting, and never lose sight of the strength within you.

With love and gratitude,
Dr. Vivian Yakpo-Newton

ACKNOWLEDGMENTS

As I close the final chapter of this book, my heart overflows with gratitude. I would not have reached this point without the unwavering love, encouragement, prayers, and support of countless souls who walked beside me during the most challenging and triumphant seasons of my life.

To Auntie Judy and Uncle Richie—thank you for stepping in with wisdom, compassion, and strength. You stood in the gap for me and the boys more times than I can count.

To my siblings, especially Kofi Yakpo and Cora Yakpo-Wetzel—your love and belief in me have meant more than words can say. Even across oceans, your presence was felt.

To my beloved African students during our time in Germany, especially Ikunna, you may not realize the light you brought into my life during a time when I needed to see hope reflected in your faces. Thank you for making me feel purposeful when my world was unraveling.

To Helen, Kate, and Connie, thank you for being my anchors. For making sure my boys and I never lacked anything, whether it was a ride, a meal, a long conversation, or just your presence. You reminded me I was never alone.

To Aba, Millicent, and Sarah—my sisters, not by blood but by bond. Thank you for standing with me, praying with me, and lifting me when I didn't have the strength to stand.

To my praying sisters—Sheila, Tina, Pam, Auntie Kathy, Marie, thank you for being my spiritual lifeline. Your prayers sustained me when words failed and only tears flowed.

To Uncle Christian Adamah, thank you for praying with me endlessly, for speaking life into my spirit, and for being a steady source of faith and encouragement through the years.

To my medical family friends, Kakra, Tony, and Jennifer: thank you for always taking the time to ensure mama received the medical care she needed back home in Accra.

To all my parenting friends, thank you for loving my boys as your own, for cheering them on, and for surrounding our family with kindness and a sense of community.

To Mama, you've always been my example of quiet strength and enduring faith. Thank you for your sacrifices, your wisdom, and your unshakable love.

To my sons, Kwame and Kwesi, thank you for being my rock. You have been my reason, my purpose, my joy. Watching you grow into the incredible men you are today has been the greatest reward of my life.

And above all, I give thanks to God—my Restorer, my Healer, my Way-Maker. Every page in this book, every tear, every triumph, and every turning point has been a testament to your grace. Thank you for restoring what was broken and turning my mourning into dancing.

This book is not just mine; it belongs to all of you who held me up, spoke life over me, and believed in the woman I could become, even when I couldn't see it myself. I am deeply, eternally grateful.

www.ingramcontent.com/pod-product-compliance
Lightning Source LLC
Chambersburg PA
CBHW070035100426
42740CB00013B/2693

* 9 7 8 1 6 3 2 9 6 8 9 0 6 *